THE RISE OF FASCISM IN BRITAIN

THE RISE OF FASCISM IN BRITAIN

FROM THE SUFFRAGE MOVEMENT TO OSWALD MOSLEY

ANTHONY J RANDALL

PEN & SWORD
HISTORY
AN IMPRINT OF PEN & SWORD BOOKS LTD
YORKSHIRE – PHILADELPHIA

First published in Great Britain in 2026 by
PEN AND SWORD HISTORY
An imprint of
Pen & Sword Books Ltd
Yorkshire – Philadelphia

Print ISBN 978 1 03618 408 7
ePUB ISBN 978 1 03618 410 0
ePDF ISBN 978 1 03618 411 7

A CIP catalogue record for this book is available from the British Library.

Typeset in Times New Roman 12/16 by
SJmagic DESIGN SERVICES, India.
Printed and bound in the UK by CPI Group (UK) Ltd.

The Publisher's authorised representative in the EU for product safety is Authorised Rep Compliance Ltd., Ground Floor, 71 Lower Baggot Street, Dublin D02 P593, Ireland.
www.arccompliance.com

For a complete list of Pen & Sword titles please contact
PEN & SWORD BOOKS LIMITED
George House, Units 12 & 13, Beevor Street, Off Pontefract Road,
Barnsley, South Yorkshire, S71 1HN, England
E-mail: enquiries@pen-and-sword.co.uk
Website: www.pen-and-sword.co.uk

or

PEN AND SWORD BOOKS
1950 Lawrence Rd, Havertown, PA 19083, USA
E-mail: uspen-and-sword@casematepublishers.com
Website: www.penandswordbooks.com

MIX
Paper | Supporting responsible forestry
FSC
www.fsc.org
FSC® C013604

DEDICATION

To Isabel, my wife for sixty years, and my two children, Hazel and Ivan – not so young now, who have supported me during the last few difficult years.

CONTENTS

Preface ix

Chapter 1 A War of Attrition 1
Chapter 2 Tiny Jackboots 15
Chapter 3 White Feathered Fools 29
Chapter 4 Women's Suffrage 43
Chapter 5 The British Fascisti 49
Chapter 6 The General Strike 61
Chapter 7 A Plethora of Parties 75
Chapter 8 The New Party 89
Chapter 9 Charisma 103
Chapter 10 Concentrating Power 109
Chapter 11 Riot and Abdication 121
Chapter 12 Regulation 18b 135
Chapter 13 End of the Affair 149

Biographical Notes 155
Index 157

PREFACE

The most important thing is to make very clear that this book is an attempt to tell the story of how fascism came so close to becoming a reality in Britain. It does not try to justify fascism, or even explain it, certainly not to support it. But it does not describe fascism in terms of disapproval so as to hide its true history. In truth, its history does not extend back even to the start of the chronology covered by this book, but is recognisable as displaying elements of its character before they were eventually codified.

There are three main features of fascism as we have come to recognise it. The subjugation of personal wellbeing to that of the nation; the disdain for parliamentary democracy and the need for experts to make decisions in its stead; a strong dynamic leader to take the helm without fear of sanction. The adoption of policies of isolationism so that the fascist nation is not drawn into wars, thereby rejecting socialism or communism, and their natural companion – internationalism.

In the early years, the word 'fascism' is not even mentioned, but is conflated with the words 'duty', 'loyalty' and 'patriotism'. The contention of this book is that it is a concept born out of a fear of socialism, rather than a desire to be governed differently. That the giving of white feathers to men who refused to volunteer during the First World War was the starting point of what we now know as fascism.

The concept of fascism, at least the early British form of fascism, can be traced back to the fight for women's suffrage and how that was sacrificed in the name of patriotism, leaving young women free to try to help the country in whatever way they thought possible – however misguided.

This study uses many source documents, mostly provincial newspapers. As many newspaper reports are syndicated it is not possible always to name the original source, but please accept this acknowledgement of the *British Newspaper Archive* as a primary source.

CHAPTER I

A WAR OF ATTRITION

The submarine *Iota*, under the command of Captain John Sirius, lay off the coast of Norfolk with the distant lights from its scattered villages twinkling off the starboard bow. The *Iota* was surface running, using its diesel engines, both to recharge its batteries and to allow it to stay in radio communication with the base station. It was about 5 am on a fine April morning, John Sirius was alone on his tiny bridge, all around was quiet, allowing him a rare opportunity to ruminate on the events that had led him to this course of action. He saw the enemy's failings quite clearly; party politics had clouded their judgement and this had finally led to war.

Heading further south the *Iota* was soon off Lowestoft, with its fleet of inshore fishing boats scattered across the water with a watchful torpedo destroyer in attendance. The *Iota* submerged, engaged electric silent running mode, and maintained periscope depth while heading still further south. By 10 am the *Iota* was lying off Essex, at the Maplin Sands, surface running and within a few hours of its planned destination, the Thames estuary. Nearing the estuary she was running at periscope depth again, and at about 1 pm she hove-to and laid in wait for a victim. That victim was the *Adela* from London, bringing frozen mutton from New Zealand to feed a working population in Britain.

The *Adela* succumbed to a single torpedo launched from the *Iota*, blowing away her starboard quarter and leaving her low in the water with her stern submerged, her cargo of mutton never to reach its intended consumers. Close behind the *Adela* came the P&O *Moldavia* followed by the P&O *Cusco* – both were sunk, denying Britain much-needed grain. Two other ships were sunk that day, the *Maid of Athens* and the *Cormorant*, bringing Captain Sirius' total number of 'kills' to five for the day – 50,000 tons consigned to the bottom of the sea. Submerged again, the *Iota* was hidden from the torpedo-boats swarming out of Sheerness.

After dark, Captain Sirius had the radio mast erected above the conning-tower and spoke to his base station and to other submarines in the eight-vessel squadron scattered around the British Isles, each with a very specific plan to follow. Captain Sirius had overall command of the squadron; it was he that had come up with the strategy and he that would be responsible for ensuring its success. The plan was simple: out-gunned and out-manoeuvred, his country had decided on a strike-and-run strategy to deny Britain the imported food that it relied upon – they would starve Britain into submission.

The next morning, yet another ship was sunk, the *Virginia*, spreading yet more grain meant for the London markets on the surface of the German ocean. With no more ships to plunder, the *Iota* headed further south, passing a German freighter, which it saluted and left undisturbed. On reaching Boulogne, in the outer harbour, Captain Sirius found three ships at anchor waiting to cross the Channel under cover of darkness. The *Caesar*, the *Pathfinder* and the *King of the East* were all sunk where they lay. Heading back to the Kent coast, the *Iota* submerged and again lay in wait for a victim.

The next ship intercepted was the *Vermondia*, out of Boston. Again, the *Iota* slipped away without being challenged. This had been Captain Sirius' strategy when he proposed the plan to his superiors. Attacks should be unannounced and without warning, no confrontation with British warships, and without risk to individual submarines within the squadron. To measure how effective the plan to starve Britain into submission was, the *Iota* surfaced alongside a small yachting party and demanded any newspapers that it had on board. The *London Courier* announced that the price of wheat in the capital had nearly doubled since the sinkings had begun.

With no ships daring to head into the Thames, the *Iota* headed west to meet up with its sister submarine, the *Kapper*, operating off the entrance into Southampton and Portsmouth, from where they then intended to travel together further west. The *Kapper*, like the *Iota*, had enjoyed some considerable success in sinking supply ships preparing to unload their foodstuffs in British ports. An engineering problem delaying *Iota*, the two submarines sailed separately to a new rendezvous point further west. Travelling alone, *Kappa* was sunk by an armed merchant ship while on the surface – using its machine gun rather than expend more torpedoes.

Meeting up with the *Delta* and the *Epsilon*, which had been operating in the Bristol Channel, the three made their way back to base. The other four submarines that were operating in northern waters similarly headed for base, well hidden from British attention. The submarines were re-armed, re-supplied and sent back on station to renew their blockade of Britain. While ashore, Captain Sirius was able to fully appreciate the effects of his siege. The price of grain in Britain had risen three-fold, there were starving crowds in the street, troops were guarding government buildings and protecting ministers from assassination attempts. Lloyd's had raised the cost of marine insurance to a prohibitive level, which meant that even fewer ships entered British waters.

The British government commandeered whatever food reached Britain and then doled it out to the population much as a garrison under siege might. After this last-ditch attempt to stabilise matters failed, the British government sued for peace. The terms were not onerous, and we did not consider that country to be a long-term enemy.

The account of Captain John Sirius' exploits serves to illustrate the radical nature of waging war, far from the gentlemanly constraints of the nineteenth century and far from the separation of military and civilian experience. The twentieth-century experience of war placed the civil population in the forefront of the battle. Men might bear arms, but women had their part to play, not only by supporting the children and old people left behind, but in encouraging their menfolk to enlist as part of the struggle. War would call for men in numbers never before seen, men would be sacrificed at the altar of a mechanised killing machine and women would support them in the factories and down the mines. The enemy would not pull its punches, nor would it hesitate to employ any tactic that would present it with victory.

The account above is, of course, entirely fictitious and appeared first in the July 1914 edition of the *Strand* magazine, one of a series of short stories by Sir Arthur Conan Doyle. This one called *Danger, Beginning the log of Captain John Sirius*, is a warning of what he felt might lie ahead if Britain were to go to war with Germany. He believed that such a war would call upon the man in the street to a greater extent than ever before. Although published only a month before war was declared, it was written eighteen months earlier, around March 1913, introducing the concept of unrestricted submarine warfare to public awareness.

The following is an extract from that story in Captain John Sirius' words as written by Sir Arthur Conan Doyle:

> Of course England will not be caught napping in such a fashion again! Her foolish blindness is partly explained by her delusion that her enemy would not torpedo merchant vessels. Common sense should have told her that her enemy will play the game that suits best that they will not inquire what they may do, but they will do it first and talk about it afterwards. The opinion of the whole world now is that if a blockade were proclaimed one may do what one can do with those who try to break it, and it was as reasonable to prevent food from reaching England in war

> time as it was for a besieger to prevent the victualling of a beleaguered fortress.

Conan Doyle's prophecy of unrestricted submarine warfare was not without its critics, some complaining that the story, in its entirety, was a slur on the readiness of Britain's navy and its ability to counter such a threat. Many believed that no country would abandon the existing Cruiser Rules, whereby submarines would only attack merchant shipping while surfaced and in plain sight. They would not attack using torpedoes, unannounced and while hidden below the water and, except in the rarest of cases, would leave them to continue their journey. Cruiser Rules were part of International Maritime Law which was generally adhered to.

Also in the words of Captain John Sirius, as written by Conan Doyle:

> Already the lines of reconstruction are evident. The first and most important is that our Party men realise that there is something more vital than their academic disputes about Free Trade or Protection, and that all theory must give way to the fact that a country is in an artificial and dangerous condition if she does not produce within her own borders sufficient food to at least keep life in her population. Whether this should be brought about by a tax upon foreign foodstuff, or by a bounty upon home products, or by a combination of the two, is now under discussion.

Conan Doyle had a long history of political campaigning, warning the public of forthcoming dangers which continued to be ignored by mainstream politicians. Such a case in point being his concerns over the Second Boer War which Britain fought from 1899 to 1902. Conan Doyle's view was that Britain should be able to call on volunteers to provide the soldiers necessary to fight the war. His opinion was shared by fellow writer Rudyard Kipling, later to travel to the Orange Free State, and one who held similar imperialistic views. Conan Doyle left for Africa in 1900 as a volunteer with the Royal Army Medical Corps (RAMC) and tended to the British sick and injured in that campaign.

Conan Doyle was not alone in predicting war; in Britain there was already a fear that Britain would be at war with Germany in the very near future. Erskine Childers, an Irish writer, published his novel *The Riddle of the Sands* in 1903. It was about a German plot to invade the east coast of Britain, and the plot, unlike that of Conan Doyle's, was foiled. It fed on a growing distrust of Germany's intentions towards Britain and the Empire. It foretold the coming of a war which would strike at Britain's entire population, men, women and children. Typical of the feelings of the time, Childers' book highlights the moral deficiency of the Germans, as against the open clarity of the British heroes.

Rudyard Kipling, ultra-conservative in his views and somewhat jingoistic in his manner of expression, certainly showed signs of racism in his writings but without intending harm to those he undermined. His political views, while being imperialistic, idealised the British Empire to the point of exercising an almost paternal care for its people. Kipling and Conan Doyle were in Africa at the same time, each one's political view being influenced by that experience.

At the conclusion of the Boer War with the signing of the Treaty of Vereeniging, it was estimated that at least 22,000 British and Colonial troops had lost their lives, similar numbers of Boer women and children in British concentration camps and nearly as many black Africans. Conan Doyle's campaigns called for mandatory inoculations for British troops serving overseas and the boiling of their drinking water, lifebelts on naval ships along with a sufficient number of lifeboats and he suggested employing new military use of large shields to protect troops in anticipated future trench warfare.

As early as 1899 he warned against Germany's ambition to become a grand power in Europe.

One significant non-military campaign was concerning the Importation of Plumage Prohibition Bill, seeking to stop the practice of killing exotic wild birds with the sole purpose of decorating women's hats. He and others were signatories of a letter to the *Spectator* newspaper.

> Sir, – We, the undersigned, have considered the Importation of Plumage Prohibition Bill. We are most heartily in accord with this measure, as we believe that it is the duty of this country to put an end to the traffic in the skins and plumes of wild birds. The evidence is abundantly clear that many rare and beautiful species now being ruthlessly exterminated, and that the trade creates a demand for the plumes of certain birds which these birds only acquire in the breeding season, thus encouraging the horrible and cruel practice of killing parent birds when the young are in the nest. The argument that the trade in prohibited feathers will not be diminished, but simply diverted to the Continent, is, in our opinion, absolutely a false one; on the contrary, we believe that the passage of this Bill will greatly strengthen the hands of the various societies and individuals who are endeavouring to promote prohibition upon the Continent. The Conference which the British Foreign Office are calling in London to consider the question of international action and prohibition has been accepted by nearly all the countries invited to attend, and though the list is not, we understand, complete, the immense majority of all countries, European and American, appears to be in accord with the proposals of the Plumage Bill. In particular, we do not believe that the passage of the Bill will bring about any shortage of work

> among those employed in the trade. A great part of the work done in connexion [sic] with this fancy plumage is performed on the Continent, and the bulk of feather-workers employed in England work, not upon wild bird plumage, but upon ostrich feathers, whose entry will be permitted, and even stimulated, by the provisions of this Bill. Also, in the natural course of things, substitutes and imitations will be found, which will divert to British labour much work that is now done in Paris and Vienna.

This issue would be of no great significance had it not been conflated with his seconding of a resolution, proposed at the annual meeting of the Royal Society for the Protection of Birds, pressing for the speedy passage of the Plumage Bill through Parliament. The seconding of the resolution was widely reported in the newspapers.

> I hope that as the white feather of cowardice is the greatest slur a man can ever wear, so may the white feather of cruelty be the greatest that a woman can wear upon her head. People sometimes spoke of the slums as showing us how near to savagery we were. After all slums were only caused by poverty: but if one sat in the upper tier of the opera and looked down to the stalls and watched the women's headgear he would often think the hats were a much stronger proof of how near we were to savagery.

The white feather is, of course, an ancient symbol of cowardice, emanating from the one-time legal pastime of cockfighting. Gamecocks were highly prized and their lineage studied and valued as carefully as that of any racehorse. Plumage was considered important insomuch as to say that the aesthetics of the bird was considered an indication of its breeding. A well-bred gamecock may bear feathers of any of a myriad of colours – but not of white. The presence of a white feather on a bird indicated a want of breeding, a lack of courage, a trait of cowardice.

The association of cowardice with the giving of a white feather was well established by the outbreak of war. In popular culture it became best known through the novel by Alfred E.W. Mason published in 1902. Under the title *The Four Feathers*, the story takes place during a colonial war when a British officer, Harry Feversham, resigns his commission just before his regiment is posted to Egypt, and is given four white feathers, three from his fellow officers, and the fourth from his fiancée, now his ex-fiancée. The four feathers are a familiar token of cowardice, well known to Mason's readership.

Feversham, admitting his cowardice, examines his motives and promises to redeem himself with his three fellow officers. He travels at his own expense to Egypt, promising that he will recover his lost friendships through acts which will erase his past cowardice. In so doing he saves one from an Omdurman prison, risking his own life in the process, and performing similar heroic acts elsewhere. His officer friends take back their white feathers and then intercede with his ex-fiancée such that their relationship is restored and they finally marry.

The moral is clearly to be seen. An act of cowardice, reflected on, can be redeemed by an act of bravery.

Alfred Mason provides a model of the English gentleman to which young men might aspire. Not entirely achievable, not entirely within reach even, but a model that many young men could be motivated by.

> They were men of one stamp; no distinction of uniform could obscure their relationship – lean-faced men, hard as iron, rugged in feature, thin-lipped, with firm chins and straight, level mouths, narrow foreheads, and the steel-blue inexpressive eyes; men of courage and resolution, no doubt, but without subtleties, or nerves, or that burdensome gift of imagination; sturdy men, a little wanting in delicacy, hardly conspicuous for intellect; to

> put it frankly, men rather stupid – all of them, in a word, first-class fighting men, but not one of them a first-class soldier.

A damning comment upon the professional soldier, but an excellent recommendation for a volunteer. A man who is tempted away from his home, wife, children etc. to sacrifice his freedom to ensure the future of his country. A real man values his own life less than he values his comfortable civilian existence. A moral man puts his own life at risk in order to defend the well-being of women – the weaker sex.

Conan Doyle was unsympathetic to the concept of conscientious objection and held the Quakers low in his estimation even though the Society of Friends, otherwise known as the Quakers, had a long history of pacifism and opposition to war. He saw their refusal to participate in armed conflict on behalf of Britain as unpatriotic and as a betrayal of their national duty. The Quakers were not alone in holding that view; most held such views based upon a religious belief but others purely on moral grounds and sought no religious doctrine to justify them.

While being unsympathetic to their views, Conan Doyle did accept that such views were consistent with Christian principles and that to stand by those principles was in itself courageous, However, principles should be able to bend in order to adapt to the reality of everyday circumstances and should not be so rigid as to become a danger to society. He believed that to ignore the practical realities of life would result in danger to the population as a whole and there must be a balance between personal liberty and the needs of society.

The idea that the rights of the individual should be sacrificed for the benefit of the nation is one which appears in the later tenets of Mussolini's introduction of fascism in Italy. Patriotism itself, with its requirement that the individual should make sacrifices for the good of the tribe, or nation, lays the very foundation of fascism without necessarily recognising it as such. That is not to equate the two, but patriotism, it could be argued, does represent one aspect of fascism.

The Church of Latter Day Saints in America, otherwise known as Mormons, held similar views to those of the Quakers. They adhered to the principle of a non-violent Zion, and so conscientious objection was a perfectly natural and justified reaction to participating in armed conflict. However, their beliefs allowed them to make exceptions to that principle should they come under direct attack. We should accept here that the concept of conscientious objection existed even though, at the outbreak of war, conscription did not exist in practise, therefore refusal to take up arms could only be a moral, not a legal, issue.

In 1914, as war is about to be declared on Germany, at least two internationally known writers have declared that Britain is embarking on a war that will be like no previous one. Tactics to be employed will consume a far greater number of lives than had ever before been anticipated, including sacrifices by women, children and the old and unrestricted submarine warfare could bring starvation to the land. With the conflation of Conan Doyle's association with the RSPB, and his views of the coming war and with the popularity of the novel *The Four Feathers*, the association of a white feather with cowardice was well established.

Rudyard Kipling's dislike for conscientious objectors can be best illustrated by quoting a poem which he wrote in 1932, long after this time. It is reflecting on a prominent conscientious objector raised to the peerage by Labour Prime Minister Ramsay MacDonald.

> Oh belted Sons of Treason
> Press onward to the Lords,
> Where six safe months in prison,
> Can win such great rewards!
>
> From Jutland to Judæa
> Bob up, ye Dead, and sing!

He'll sit with wicked Beatty,
And Allenby and Byng!

Through toil and tribulation
And tumult of our war,
He sought the consummation
Of peace forever more.

A million fell beside him,
By land and air and sea,
In order to provide him
With breakfast, lunch and tea!

By 1914 the British people had, for some time, anticipated a war with Germany, as that country's expansion plans were mirrored by the sizes of their two empires. Britain's empire was spread around the world, providing both food and natural resources to be brought back to the homeland. Germany's empire was not spread worldwide, and its agricultural production was less valuable. Much of the British Empire held dominion status, while the German Empire was primarily subjugated. Security of the British Empire was in the hands of the individual expat farmer, while the German Army was left to police that empire.

In having such a widespread empire, Britain had relied on the strength of its navy to defend its empire against invasion. The expected route to war was by sea, and Britain had watched while Germany had strengthened its own navy in anticipation of standing face-to-face with the British fleet. Erskine Childers, in his book, had anticipated a sea-borne confrontation, in this case an armada of troop-carrying barges being towed across the German ocean, or North Sea as we now know it. Similarly a sea-borne conflict in Conan Doyle's fantasy this time employed submarines. But, thanks to an impulsive student in Serbia, the much-anticipated war with Germany was a land war – for which Britain was ill-prepared.

Britain had pursued a policy of internationalism, perhaps owing to her influence across the entire world, trading with many countries, dominions, colonies and a great number of unaligned nations. This reliance upon trade, especially for foodstuffs, as Conan Doyle showed, was also Britain's vulnerability. Many were of the opinion that isolationism would make Britain more able to rely upon her domestic productivity to sustain herself against a threat such as she now faced. This was another tenet of fascism, although not so named at this point.

Attitudes in Germany were expressed by its ambassador in London.

> Everywhere amongst the cultivated classes in Germany it is laid down as a dogma that the German Empire does not play in world politics the part which is her due. The great organs spread everywhere the doctrine, at once dangerous and irritant, that German prestige is diminishing. The patriotic demand action.

As a time of peace became a time of war, the prospect of war became a reality. Conan Doyle predicted that this would not be a war where the soldier sailed away, his wife or sweetheart waving her handkerchief toward a distantly retreating ship's wake. It would involve the entire nation, young men looking for adventure, young women crying for their lost love, mothers and fathers mourning their sons. This would become a war of the people, not just of the warrior. Everyone must make their sacrifice.

CHAPTER 2

TINY JACKBOOTS

War was declared between Britain and Germany on 4 August 1914. The anticipation of war between the two countries had been a constant talking point amongst the political classes for some time, if not an everyday subject of conversation within the general population, and preparations were in place to be ready for such an event. The outbreak of war had been expected to be brought about as the result of a naval attack of some kind on the east coast, perhaps Norfolk, else through Scapa Flow in the north; or perhaps as the result of a submarine blockade as predicted by Sir Arthur Conan Doyle.

Events were very different than had been anticipated. The assassination of Archduke Franz Ferdinand, nephew of Emperor Franz Josef and heir to the Austro-Hungarian Empire, set off a chain reaction in Europe that ended up with Britain sending an army to defend Belgium, under its treaty obligations, from an occupying German force. When the British and German armies met, the active running war became a long and protracted trench war stalemate with an enormous loss of manpower such that, again, Sir Arther Conan Doyle's prediction seemed a little less fanciful than before.

Unlike Germany, the British Army was a volunteer force, made up of those who were professional soldiers; likewise the navy and its sailors. As war approached there was considerable anti-German feeling in the country, which prompted men to volunteer for service. The German people were seen as cruel and barbarous and that Britain was defending 'poor little Belgium' against the Hun, their final target being France – a little too close to the Channel ports to be comfortable.

Conan Doyle's other great cause was the need for a tunnel running beneath the English Channel, the building of which he had promoted for many years. He admitted that in the scenario that he wrote of in his short story about the submarine blockade, *Danger*, it would have been of little practical use but, if Marseilles were not in enemy hands, the transport of food coming through that Mediterranean port would have been of considerable help, let alone the men and machinery heading for the Continent. He claimed that to reject the idea of building such a tunnel would be considered as national stupidity.

Duty to king and country was still a strong driving force, even though the call for socialism was becoming stronger, and there was little doubt that God would be on Britain's side in the coming conflict – after all, it was a well-known fact that God's mother tongue was English, rather than German. It was not entirely easy to come to terms with the fact that King George, and the rest of the royal family, were as German as Kaiser Wilhelm II. Those calling for socialism were equally uneasy about Tsar Nicholas II being similarly descended from Queen Victoria.

At the outbreak of war, the Women's Social and Political Union (WSPU) abandoned its activities for the duration. The group, campaigning for women's suffrage, were politically unaligned and operated under the leadership of Emmeline Pankhurst and her daughter Christabel. The term *suffragette* was a derogatory one first coined by a *Daily Mail* journalist to describe WSPU members whose activities were either illegal or anti-social. Members of the WSPU liked the term and adopted it, believing it identified them as more dynamic and determined than was implied with the more mundane, if correct, name.

During the immediate pre-war years, the suffragettes became even more militant than earlier, including taking part in riots, civil disobedience, criminal damage and even bombing. Upon being gaoled, they took part in hunger strikes and were force fed – a cruel way for a government to treat its women. Emmeline and Christabel established themselves in Paris and from there managed the progress of the WSPU's suffrage campaign. It was in Paris that Sylvia Pankhurst, another daughter, formalised her split from the WSPU for organising a competing pressure group.

This split was over her obsession to incorporate socialism into the fight for women's suffrage. Up to that point, the WSPU had remained free of any specific political alliance. Sylvia's connections with socialism were incompatible with the WSPU's policy in two aspects; the first because of their insistence on non-alliance, the second because many of its supporters harboured a growing hostility to socialism and an increasing distrust of the far left, particularly communism.

Why the WSPU abandoned its campaign for the duration of fighting was, on the face of it, in consideration of the need to rally in support of the greater threat to the government in having to fight both at home and abroad. There is the greater reason, however, that a great deal of public support would be lost should the campaign be considered as disloyal. There was a general view amongst women that the cause was just, even if the individual woman did not want to take part and surely the tacit support of men would fade away should the WSPU be thought of as disloyal.

A more realistic view might be that the WSPU recognised that they could not fight for the country's support and divide the government's growing empathy towards their demands while a far greater danger threatened. The fight for women's suffrage had been going for ten years under the WSPU, and to date had no major breakthrough in the world of power and influence. Better, perhaps, to rack up a little kudos, with no appreciable effort, and to put country before self – another tenet of fascism.

Emmeline Pankhurst energetically threw herself into the patriotic support of the war effort as she had previously done to support the women's suffrage movement. In return the government released all the WSPU members who had been detained because of their militant behaviour, repaid by the suffragettes loudly supporting voluntary recruitment into the armed forces. Many of the younger WSPU members accepted their new role as government supporters but were hungry for the excitement of militancy. Many joined groups such as the Red Cross where there was an opportunity to work abroad, near to the front line, in such foreign places as France or Serbia.

Other young women members, cast adrift as it were by the abandoned militancy of the WSPU, returned to their mundane suburban lives. Within them was a dissatisfaction with their sedentary lives, for which they held the assumed masculine power over the feminine to be largely responsible. Some reconciled this view with reality to the extent that they were of the opinion that men, all men, should bear the burden of fighting to counterbalance the sacrifice that women had experienced for generations past. Their frustration at being denied suffrage in a male-dominated world meant yet another round of masculine-led conflict, in which the woman's role would be that of a helpless victim.

The masculine and feminine roles have existed across the generations, in part by traditional social conventions, and confirmed by male-dominated actions that have tended to reinforce those conventions. Physical strength has played its part in matters of work and recreation: playing at soldiers and boxing were as foreign to the traditional girl as playing at being a washerwoman or needlework were to her male counterpart. Young suffragettes would point out that the relative intellects were not so different, and that the female mind was as capable of rational thought as was the male mind. Their call for women's suffrage was as much to do with equality of opportunity to contribute as it was to vote.

The British government quickly realised that if Conan Doyle's predictions about the loss of lives were realised, then the number of regular soldiers and sailors would need to be supplemented by volunteers. The government was supported in this view, not only by the WSPU, but by many ex-suffragettes, now stood down, but of that same opinion. This view was given legitimacy by Lord Kitchener, the Secretary of State for War, issuing his famous poster calling for volunteers. His call was answered, but there was always the need for more, and there were militant young women available to help. At this time they were sitting at home, ruing their loss of a structure under which to work, when along came Admiral Charles Penrose-Fitzgerald.

Charles Penrose-Fitzgerald was 73 years old and had already retired from the navy when the war began in 1914. During his career he had achieved some success as a writer, having penned a biography of Admiral Rooke. After retirement he had been asked to write a piece on British naval policy for the German magazine *Deutsche Revue*. Although writing in English he had no influence on the German translation which, he claimed, somewhat exaggerated his statements which were then used by the Germans to encourage support for their speeded up shipbuilding programme.

In retirement, Penrose-Fitzgerald lived in Folkestone, a port town in the south-east, directly opposite France. It was from this port that many British soldiers embarked for the front line. With no formal backing from any authority, he called a meeting in the town, attracting a number of young women, evidently a number holding militant views. There had been pressure groups in existence since the turn of the century, pushing for the introduction of compulsory military training for all young men, to match the conscription that was to be found in other countries. One such group was the National Service League (NSL), founded by conservative politicians, although not official Conservative policy.

As a note of interest, the NSL held some of its meetings at the reading rooms in Crowborough in Sussex, where one of the local residents was Arthur Conan Doyle. Not far off was Batemans, the family home of Rudyard Kipling in Burwash, just a dozen miles away. Crowborough is no more than 50 miles from Folkestone and both of these men had motor cars. At one of the NSL meetings at Crowborough in 1912, it was emphasised the call was for training of young men to be in a state of readiness, rather than for their immediate conscription.

At the meeting, Penrose-Fitzgerald addressed his words to the men of Folkestone, who he warned of 'a danger awaiting them far more terrible than they could meet in battle'. He warned that if they were found 'idling and loafing tomorrow' then they would be confronted by 'a fearsome lady brandishing a white feather'. The meeting was reported widely, the article below from the *Woolwich Gazette*.

> Thirty Folkestone women have banded themselves together to present a white feather to every young "slacker" found loafing about the Leas or indifferent to their country's need, just to remind them that British men are fighting and dying across the Channel. Admiral Penrose-Fitzgerald, who out of seventy-three years of life has served his country for fifty-one years, is the force behind the "white feather" movement. On Sunday morning he made speeches from the two bandstands on the Leas. "It is all very well," he said, "to call upon the working men to join the Army as they are doing, but it is the duty of people who have public-school and university education to set the example. I warn the young men of Folkestone – the idle ones – that there is a danger awaiting them far more terrible than anything they can meet in battle, and that is, if they are found idling and loafing to-morrow they will be presented by a lady with a white feather".

At a meeting of the NSL, of which Penrose-Fitzgerald was a member, they were confident that their warnings of Britain being unready for conflict had been proved correct. Volunteers had stepped forward, but the hundred thousand so far recruited was less than the half-million men required. Lord Roberts, their president, urged the men of Kent to step forward and set an example to the rest of the country. Again, the prospect of women shaming men into volunteering was raised using the warning that 'Petticoats were wanted for all able-bodied young men who had not yet joined the Navy or Army'.

The reaction to events in Folkestone was quite unexpected. One newspaper reader commentated that many young men, without one spark of patriotism, were quite content to take their ease and make their money while others were enduring untold privations in the trenches. Men were offering their lives freely to secure a continuance of ease and freedom for their mothers, fathers and sisters. It was difficult to reconcile the men serving in Belgium and France as being from the same stock as those of the 'white feather lot'. Such men cut such contemptible figures. Another was doubtful that any young man who was capable of turning a deaf ear to the threat of the Order of the White Feather would respond as anticipated.

The choice of language is interesting: on the one hand those who answered the call were referred to as 'men', while those who failed to do so, were referred to as 'youths'. From the very start, the language of persuasion was nuanced with sexual innuendo without specifically referring to the fact. The implication being that enthusiasm to enlist indicated sexual prowess or maturity, while to refuse indicated immaturity and unproven virility. The use of words like lounging and petticoats only added to the insult. Their challenge from the weaker sex only reinforced such a view.

Further along the coast from Folkestone, in Deal, the town crier was brought out to announce to the town that any young men, with no one dependent on them, would be presented with the Order of the White Feather. By not volunteering they stood accused of shirking their duty to support the Union Flag. While this was happening, young women had been touring the beaches and promenades, presenting white goose feathers to young men found lolling around, and fixing them to their coat lapels and hat-bands.

Not all views were as positive. Some thought that the Order of the White Feather would be quite ineffective against the men of England, which is not a military nation but rather a seafaring and business one and, as such, looks to its navy to give it a real sense of security. An intelligent recognition of the facts of the situation, and a real attempt to deal with them, would produce better results than by the issuing of insults. While few could be considered heroes, it does not necessarily follow that most are cowards. One letter from one of the white feather brigade of women, elicited a response.

> If these females would employ themselves knitting the socks, belts, etc., for which Lord Kitchener is appealing, they would be serving their country a great deal better than in hurting the feelings of those who are infinitely less cowardly themselves. Protected by "skirts" from the liability of serving, it is easy to jeer at others. It is creatures like these who make one inclined to uphold the view of some anti-suffragettes that there must be a third sex. If the particular female in question was married I could quite imagine that her husband has gone to the war!

Nonconformists were positively encouraged to volunteer, it being a righteous war such as Oliver Cromwell fought. One correspondent expressed the opinion that Germany had treated the Christian law as less than nothing and that the German 'code of conduct was infinitely baser than that of the savage'. He believed that when the facts were clearly set out, men would abhor the stain of cowardice more than the risk of death.

Some men would need to remain civilians, of course. Those in occupations that were vital to the country's wellbeing, not only those that were contributing to the war effort – schoolmasters for example. The chairman of Nuneaton council said that everyone who could serve should enlist, but by staying in Nuneaton they would be showing greater courage. Suffering public criticism for the good of the children meant they would be making a greater sacrifice than by going to France. In reality, of course, it was quite simple for those responsible for ensuring that children were educated to relax the rules whereby women who chose to marry were not forced to retire. In many schools this resulted in a staff much populated by married women teachers.

In fact any number of men could substantiate a similar claim. Policemen, doctors, vicars, dentists – the list is endless. In order to maintain a fighting army overseas, a significant number must remain behind in order to keep the country working so that they have something tangible for which to return home. Men had to remain behind to sweep the roads, bury the dead, rebuild the houses, mine the coal and fight the fires. Some of that work could be undertaken by women, and so they did, but some of the skills required could not be taught in a few weeks or months. Some skills took years to learn – some, a lifetime.

Some critics of the women bestowing white feathers had a simple solution to the brigade's problem – lead by example. Many in the correspondence columns suggested that the women of the White Feather Brigade – who they associated with the suffragettes – should, rather than shame young men into enlisting, step forwards themselves. It was an empty argument as neither the army nor navy would accept women for military service on the front line. A fact well known to all, but no more pertinent than might be heard in any public bar from armchair generals.

Many young women did seek active service by joining the Red Cross, Volunteer Ambulance Corps, Scottish Women's Hospitals, or any number of organisations which attracted young adventurous women. Some featured overseas locations, often near to the front line, and offered near battlefield experiences. Many young women who had previously been a member of, or at least supported, the suffragettes, chose these less disciplined services. Certainly some of the units of the Scottish Women's Hospitals offered an environment where women could enjoy same-sex relationships without too many problems.

Referring to one unit of the Scottish Women's Hospitals, this author wrote previously of this being a feature not only of the rank and file, but also of their leaders.

> This all-female unit, again, had its origins in the suffragist movement with an easy acceptance of same sex relationships, such as that between Dr Lilian Cooper and her companion Josephine Bedford who "had worshipped each other from the early days of their youth". Cooper and Bedford had both returned from Australia to contribute to the British war effort. Bedford, not medically trained, travelled with the *American Unit* only because Dr Cooper was unable to function properly without her. Lacking a formal role, Bedford unofficially took charge of the motor department; vehicles, chauffeurs, tools and accessories.

More literary names came forward to support the White Feather Brigade, although not being a single organisation, it manifested itself in a plethora of disguises. Baroness Orczy was a well-known author, famous for writing *The League of The Scarlet Pimpernel*, among other works. She was an enthusiast by way of the Women of England's Active Service League, which she formed to bestow white feathers upon reluctant recruits, and was a supporter of British imperialism and militarism and managed to recruit over 20,000 to her cause. Conversely another novelist, Mary Augusta Ward, writing under the name Mrs Humphry Ward, was specifically anti-suffragette but was still a keen supporter of the White Feather Brigade.

To Baroness Orczy, refusing to be seen in public with a man out of uniform symbolically denied him access to the female body. In effect, denying him the sexual recognition that he sought, a form of coercion that isolated him from enjoying a normal sexual existence, thereby bringing public shame down upon him. The assumption she wished to promote was that the wearing of a military uniform implied sexual prowess in him who wore it, or at least did not suggest the opposite.

The bravado displayed in the first months of the war meant that groups of women, emboldened by their novelty value and seeming public support, delivered white feathers to their victims personally – later this would become an anonymous act. The technique would be to approach a candidate in the street and to then, under the guise of flattery or familiarity, pin or otherwise attach the white feather to his person. Then to abuse him of his failings, both as a citizen and as a man, implying that his supposed manly qualities were really those of a defenceless woman.

The idea did not seem to occur to the White Feather Brigade that any man out of uniform on whom their eye fell could be legitimate in being so dressed. Their victim could be a boy, an invalid, a policeman, a doctor, a schoolmaster or follow any one of a number of occupations. He could be a soldier home on leave, a wounded soldier recovering from an injury, a victim of shellshock, or in any of a myriad of conditions. With no information except their own conjecture, they were quite indiscriminating in their search for volunteers.

As a reminder of the fervour with which the ladies pursued their righteous cause, the following is a first-hand account by one so challenged, and quoted by A.M. Kilday and D.S. Nash in their 2017 book *Shame and Modernity in Britain.*

> On my way to work one morning a group of women surrounded me. They started shouting and yelling at me, calling me all sorts of names for not being a soldier! Do

> you know what they did? They struck a white feather in my coat, meaning I was a coward. Oh I did feel dreadful, so ashamed. I went to the recruiting office. The sergeant there couldn't stop laughing at me, saying things like "Looking for your father, sonny?", and "Come back next year when the war's over!" Well, I must have looked so crestfallen that he said "Let's check your measurements again." You see, I was five foot six inches and only about eight and a half stone. This time he made me out to be six feet tall and twelve stone, at least, that is what he wrote down. All lies of course – but I was in.

During this early stage of the war, Emmeline and Christabel Pankhurst toured Britain, drumming up support for the voluntary recruitment campaign, and handed out white feathers to every young man they encountered wearing civilian dress. At this time the Pankhursts began to consider the possibility of imposing some form of conscription on both men and women. The issue never proceeded beyond being a matter for discussion, considering that the persuasion of men to join the army was the best way that young women could perform a national service.

Here again we see that one of the main tenets of fascism is met, nation before self. Never before have we witnessed an army consisting largely of volunteers. In previous times soldiering was considered as an occupation which offered a wage, much as working on the farm, or down the mine, or in the factory might: for the officer riding as a cavalryman with its accompanying status, sitting behind a desk in Whitehall, perhaps as a prelude to gaining an inheritance. Never had service to the crown been offered so altruistically, so freely.

In 1914 men had enlisted as volunteers in response to calls of 'King and Country', while others had been shamed into doing so. There were still some social elements to be overcome: King George V not being a charismatic leader as required by fascism and, for the time being, politicians not being usurped by experts, nor any suggestion that parliamentary democracy should make way for dictatorship. But already we see the metaphoric jackboot of the tyrant being worn on the tiny foot of the suffragette, posing as a self-righteous member of the White Feather Brigade.

Admiral Charles Penrose-Fitzgerald appears to have played no further part in the White Feather Brigade, other than in its formation, and died peacefully in 1921, still in Folkestone.

CHAPTER 3

WHITE FEATHERED FOOLS

The movement that stemmed from Admiral Penrose-Fitzgerald's meeting in Folkestone was never established as a formal organisation. Certainly the aims and ambitions were accepted by its disciples but were never codified as might be a religion. There was never a central structure, membership of which might be able to offer an insight as to the number of members, their politics or the organisation's constitution, something which contained a list of members or if indeed it were made up entirely of women.

The White Feather Brigade was never a single entity, but rather an idea that any number of individuals adopted as their own. The idea was powerful enough to grasp the imagination of young women around the country but no attempt was made to co-ordinate their individual activities under a single banner. There was a common purpose, which was to enhance and support General Kitchener's campaign to increase voluntary enlistment into the army. Beneath this single aim there were also a number of secondary considerations in the mix – not all complimentary, one to another.

Patriotism was the single most obvious reason for taking an active role within the movement. The enthusiasm for war was quite widespread within the general population. There was considerable anti-German feeling within Britain, having been bombarded with propaganda in the British newspapers for some time. The common view was of Germany, characterised by the spiked helmet of a Prussian officer, threatening the virtue of a chaste English maiden.

Such an image contributed not only fear of what could be awaiting Britain's female population, but also affrontery that such events might be even contemplated.

Of the political events that had led to state of war, the young women of the White Feather Brigade were generally less aware. Events in far away Serbia, and the domino-like tumbling of international treaties, were of less impact than the sentiment of 'poor little Belgium' invaded by the 'Hun'. The forthcoming conflict was a 'call to arms' by King George V, supported by the British government and by the Loyal Opposition; that call went out for volunteers to join the army and the White Feather Brigade was encouraging the faint hearted to answer that call.

Solidarity with sons, brothers, husbands and sweethearts was another driving force behind joining the movement. By the end of 1914 nearly a million men had volunteered for active service. Such was the response that the government formed what became known as Pals companies, allowing groups of men with local connections not only to enlist together, but to serve together. Perhaps the best known of these is the one formed around the men of Sandringham House in Norfolk and supported by the king and queen.

The Sandringham Company had been formed in 1906 as part of the 5th Battalion Norfolk Regiment, Territorial Force and known as Company 'E', under Frank Beck, the king's land agent. The company was manned by gardeners, grooms and other household staff – a true Pals company. They went together to Gallipoli where they, and many of the 5th Battalion, were killed in action. The entire Norfolk Territorial Force was drawn from companies similarly formed.

The women's involvement in the White Feather Brigade enabled them to satisfy their need to offer help to the men in their struggle, by making sure they would not be alone, but among their friends and colleagues. Even if the new recruits were not personally known to them, every son, brother, husband and sweetheart's odds of injury or death would be lengthened by the swollen numbers. Although that argument is flawed, to the individual woman left behind, it contained an irrefutable logic which overcome mathematical probability.

With their menfolk overseas the women were left at home, some to work in what would otherwise be their men's world, but for wives with young children to care for, backing the White Feather Brigade with deeds, or simply with moral support, enabled them to feel they were 'doing their bit' for their loved ones overseas. Many would end the war as widows, or otherwise bereaved, and this very public and militant action would provide justification for them, having given up their menfolk as Kitchener had requested.

The human cost of the war extended far beyond the individual families who had suffered loss. The scale of bereavement and social disruption also had profound political consequences, shaping attitudes towards future international conflict and Britain's place in the world. Isolationism was a very attractive concept, and yet another building block in the construction of fascism, with internationalism being associated with socialism and thus entering into agreements, and obligations, to other countries.

An opportunity for adventure was the most practical and plausible of these secondary motives. With the suspension of the women's suffrage movement in 1914, there was a vast body of young women with a taste for militant action who suddenly found themselves forcibly inactive. Many of the suffragettes found active roles in the many and various women's organisations being formed, mostly involving some degree of nursing, but others were not so happy, simply being one cog in a strictly discipled machine.

One such young woman, not an active suffragette but sympathetic to their cause, was Rotha Lintorn-Orman, who would play a large part in Britain's post-war political future. She joined the Scottish Women's Hospital as an ambulance driver, serving in Serbia close to the front line, and experiencing a surfeit of adventure. Finally she was invalided out, suffering from malaria, and then helped fight the Great Fire of Thessaloniki in Greece. On finally returning to Britain she worked with the Red Cross before, at the end of the war, finally turning to politics.

For many young women, still economically shackled to their parents, the White Feather Brigade offered the freedom to rebel against the constraints of the 'establishment' while acting within the parental boundaries previously imposed. By being part of the White Feather Brigade they were not pushing against the family rules established during their suffragette days. They were going into the street, acting on their own initiative and risking public rejection of their views, in the name of what they considered to be a just cause. Perhaps it would be unkind to say that at the end of each day they ate at home and went to sleep in a comfortable bed and then awoke the next morning ready for the fight ahead.

These various secondary motivations were not easy bedfellows, indeed combinations such as solidarity and adventure were quite at odds with each another. Showing support for a son, brother, husband or sweetheart by urging others to enlist must have been viewed as having more gravity of purpose than simply making a public display of assumed cowardice of their fellow man. The young mother could have had little patience with those whose goal was only to beat the drum of imperialism a little louder.

The overarching motivation, while fully recognising the individual reasons for joining the White Feather Brigade, was the securing of women's suffrage. True, the Pankhursts had halted direct action at the outbreak of war, but the desire was still present in women's minds and still needed to be considered with every pseudo-political move made. The rank and file of the suffrage movement, some of whom were also the wives or sweethearts of those serving, while others were simply patriotic or looking for adventure, needed to retain their revolutionary zeal and not lose sight of the real prize.

On an individual level it afforded every woman the advantage of being the arbiter of every man's conscience. It was women's time to dictate to men what those obligations were; what their role was to be. For years women had been told that, as the weaker sex, their place in the world was defined by their position relative to men – to their father or to their husband. In proclaiming membership of the White Feather Brigade, women claimed the right to dictate to men what was expected of them, perhaps a little obscure but, when they failed to measure up, they were challenged by their feminine counterparts on their masculinity.

Masculinity was defined by the women of the White Feather Brigade, who associated masculinity with voluntarily enlisting, and so to the wearing of khaki. The general feeling was that in denying women the vote, men had implied that the female sex were unworthy, or incapable, of playing a full part in the affairs of the country. This was an opportunity to point out that, by not answering the call to arms, men could also show themselves unworthy to play such a role. Women took on the task of deciding on a spurious set of parameters, judging men according to them, and then pronouncing their guilt or innocence by way of the giving of white feathers.

The White Feather Brigade were supported in this by the War Propaganda Bureau, based in Wellington House on Buckingham Gate. This was headed by Liberal MP Charles Masterman, with fellow writers such as Arthur Conan Doyle, Arnold Bennett, John Masefield, H.G. Wells and others recruited to lend their voices. As well as the famous posters proclaiming Kitchener's call to enlist, they were also responsible for posters showing British women, and their children, advising their husbands to 'GO', and children asking their father 'What did you do in the WAR, daddy?'

Men not in khaki were shamed by militant young women bestowing white feathers on them. Handed to them in public, their shame was there to be seen by friends and passers-by. They were identified as being less of a man than others who had volunteered; as missing qualities of protectiveness that were the very essence of masculinity in the early years of the twentieth century; by implication, being less than a man who was worthy of the love of a woman, with its unspoken sexual connotations. The message was not of duty to king and country, but of sexual prowess.

There is a final consideration in the possible motives that were brought into play during this time – that of a straightforward gender war. While male homosexuality was against the law, female homosexuality, or inversion, was not. There were many examples of women living as a married couple, not least in the women's suffrage movement, and the many non-governmental volunteer organisations that looked to that movement for support. The possibility that such gender antagonism played its part in the motives of the White Feather Brigade cannot be discounted.

The simple criterion of whether or not a man was wearing khaki was open to misunderstandings, as earlier discussed. While some voices were raised against the very idea of public shaming, criticism was also mounting against the day-to-day implementation of the process. Letters were published in the newspapers that told of the consequences of bestowing white feathers inappropriately, of those who had done or were doing their duty, to those who by any natural justice should be exempt and to those who were not emotionally strong enough to bear such shame.

Amongst instances reported, there were a number of men who were targeted in error by the young women of the White Feather Brigade, and while many men were devastated to be so challenged, some were keen to put them right, perhaps in stronger language than reported here.

> There are members of the White Feather Brigade at Southsea. These young ladies in their enthusiasm for recruiting Lord Kitchener's Army make awkward mistakes at times. A Dockyard workman who has been kept hard [at it] ever since the war began, working late every night, and sometimes all through the night, went for a week-end stroll along the sea front at East Southsea, and, being tired, sat down on one of the seats. A "White Feather" lady came up and politely handed him a white feather as a hint that his proper place was at the seat of war. The man in very plain terms explained his position, with a hint that the lady would do well in future to mind her own business. On discovering her error she had the grace to apologise.

The most devastating of outcomes was reported in July 1915 when an inquest was held into the death of Charles Roberts, a taxi driver from Ealing, who had shot himself. Roberts had previously volunteered for the army, but had been rejected because of a weak heart. He was subsequently taunted by young women, and called a coward for his lack of a khaki uniform until, in perfect misery, he took his own life. The coroner's opinion was that the women's behaviour was abominable and should not be allowed to happen again. He described them as 'silly young women' who should be ashamed of themselves, and hoped that the practice of making life unbearable for men who had tried to do their duty would soon be put a stop to.

A similar mistake happened outside the Tally Ho public house in East Finchley, when a white feather was anonymously placed in the cap of Lance-Corporal H.J. Wilding who was home on furlough. Instead of being shamed, Wilding became angry at having been served in that manner, and a fight developed, resulting in one man being seriously hurt and transported to hospital. The local magistrate was equally considerate of the situation and told Wilding that he was free to return to France, and that he would hear no more of the matter so long as the injured man made a full recovery – if he died then Wilding would be brought back to answer for it.

Other instances of young women presenting white feathers to men out of uniform had lesser consequences. One man, so bestowed, had recently received the DCM and was traveling by train to the West Country in order to recuperate. A young man, given the white feather in a restaurant, was publicly upset, only to leave the restaurant shortly after, revealing that one of his legs had been shot away.

In the midst of the campaign to boost voluntary recruitment, humour was not abandoned. A tale of an encounter with the White Feather Brigade was recounted in newspapers on 1 April 1915.

> They were three young men, military age, and quite obviously fit and well, but there was a deplorable lack of anything like khaki in their attire. It was in Oxford Street that Miss Fluffy met them, and bravely held them up, though they were three to one.
>
> "Do you mind," said Miss Fluffy, in her sweetest voice, "if I give each of you a white feather?"
>
> "Not at all," said the spokesman of the party, and the feathers were handed round and accepted with smiles.
>
> Somehow Miss Fluffy felt that her first assault on the enemy's position had miscarried. There was no burning blush of shame on any one of those youthful cheeks.
>
> "You ought to be serving your King and country," said Miss Fluffy resentfully.
>
> "We're doing our best, you know", said the spokesman deprecatingly.
>
> "But how can you be when you're not in khaki?" demanded the lady.

> "Well, you see, we're not expected to wear uniform during the holidays," was the response. "We're not really officers; we're only cadets from a place called Sandhurst. Perhaps you've heard of it?"
>
> Then it was Miss Fluffy's turn to blush, and she did it handsomely. But it is too much to hope that she will give up her self-imposed task. It is patriotic, and, after all, the three cadets are now possessed of three excellent pipe-cleaners.

There were calls to Parliament that the excesses of the White Feather Brigade be curtailed. The Home Secretary was asked specifically if he would direct the police to charge the young women for behaviour likely to cause a breach of the peace. In reply, the Home Secretary said that, although he personally found their activities objectional and unlikely to assist recruitment, the police had not received a single complaint on which to act. Nor did he feel that such actions as those mentioned would necessarily lead to a breach of the peace.

In an attempt to mitigate the misdirected activities of the White Feather Brigade, the government did issue a silver badge to be awarded to servicemen who had received injuries and which made it impossible for them to return to active service. Each badge was individually numbered, and records carefully maintained, so that it obtained a certain authenticity, displayed on the right breast of a civilian suit. This, of course, made little impact on the number of men wrongly accused but prevented some of the worst wrongs being imposed. One newspaper announced it thus:

> To meet the growing nuisance and menace of the white feather, the government may issue a new badge. It will be distinct from the King's Badge, and will be given to officers and men who have come out of the Services on

> health grounds, under circumstances that do not entitle them to the King's Badge. Thus, every ex-serviceman will have protection against white-feather distributers and reproaches for not being in uniform.

As 1915 came to its end, the need for still more volunteers to enlist became a matter of urgency. When war was declared in August 1914, nearly a million men had volunteered by the end of the year, but as 1915 progressed, the rate of enlistment declined. This was the point that the NSL came to the fore yet again. The NSL had been campaigning for compulsory military training since 1902, but such a radical move had never acquired popular support, although it was reckoned to have a total membership of nearly 100,000 by the time war was declared.

Even at this early stage of the war, we can recognise traits within the psyche of the White Feather Brigade that appear again and again when the very essence of fascism is introduced. The basic tenet of the young women who spread their message across the country is that the interests of the nation should take precedence over those of the individual, and that damage to the interest of the individual should be simply accepted as collateral damage for the greater good. During a campaign where simply increasing the number of volunteers enlisting is of the greatest importance, some individual interests must be overridden.

Within the White Feather Brigade we see a militant group of young ladies, loyal to their king and country and, although not rich, can be considered as 'not poor'. They will, in the main, hold conservative views which value the British Empire on an imperial level, rather than as a simple economic asset, and will regard loyalty to their leader as paramount. During wartime their leader was undoubtedly the king by default of his title. Perhaps his second in command was Lord Kitchener, working as his spokesman to the people.

While the initial response to the war had been a generally optimistic one, that it would be all over by Christmas, with Germany left defeated, after Mons, and the rout of the British Expeditionary Force, the beginning of a protracted and stationary period took control of events. The call to volunteer and teach the Germans the error of their ways became a call to volunteer to stop the Germans from snatching victory from Britain by overrunning a depleted army. The country began to adopt a siege mentality.

The young women of the White Feather Brigade could no longer prompt those not in khaki that enlistment promised adventure, glamour and the undying love and gratitude of a devoted wife or sweetheart. Those still wearing civvies were well aware of what awaited them in France – mud, cold and the prospect of an unenviable death in a foreign country. Egos in late 1915 were not as fiercely protected as they had been a year previously, and the shaming in public became a little easier to bear.

Despite the earlier detractors, Conan Doyle's vision of the future was being proved correct. The war was consuming soldiers at an alarming rate, replacements were being required simply to maintain the numbers at the front. The troops wounded and killed were greater than the enlistment of volunteers could keep up with and the available reservoir of young men becoming old enough to legally enlist was but a drop in the ocean. The German threat had not come from the sea where Britain ruled the waves, but from the land, where tradition and strength played second fiddle to the numbers that could be commanded,

Conan Doyle's warnings of a blockade of Britain from the sea were played out before a native population which had grown used to obtaining its food from all over the world. The Royal Navy had trained to fight a surface war, but submarine warfare fell outside its usual remit. The security of the British Empire was well established by its far-flung nature. However as a source of production its remoteness was its strength – its weakness was the bottleneck created in the waters around Britain. All the food and oil in the world, scattered across the waters of the Western Approaches, were worth nothing.

The White Feather Brigade spread its influence across the Dominions of the British Empire, particularly in Australia and Canada. What seemed a good move in prompting men to volunteer for service in support of the 'old country' changed to criticism when the indiscriminate shaming of individuals resulted in harm. However, the campaign had its successes, particularly in sending men to Gallipoli where they joined with parts of the Norfolk Regiment, and Captain Beck's Sandringham Company, and suffered terrible losses.

It would be interesting to know whether these young women, either in Britain or the Dominions, in search of men to shame, ever considered the reality of what they were preaching. Although they saw their actions as patriotic, they were placing the interest of the country before those of the men they challenged. In a world where the interests of the nation took precedence over its citizens, the shadow of a more authoritarian force was becoming acceptable. That authoritarian force was not to come from the elected government of the day, but from a group who felt that they, and they alone, held the secret of how to cure the world's ills.

Finally, a comment on how the 'man in the street' viewed the shaming of his fellow worker. It recognised that it may not be him refusing to fight for his country, but that his country rejected him as not good enough. It might be assumed that each man dressed in khaki had passed the test of loyalty set by Lord Kitchener. In fact it was more likely that each man wearing civilian clothes had been rejected by his country as not being worthy of wearing khaki – a slap in the face – an insult compounded by the unwanted attentions of white-feathered fools.

> Mr Percy W. Brace, now engaged in London, has a clear record of endeavour to enlist, having been medically

examined four or five times, but unfortunately rejected. Like many others he is subject to the jeers of khaki enthusiasts, white-feathered fools. and enlistment cranks, and complains bitterly of what is virtually persecution. Some day it may dawn upon the victims of khaki fever that the man who is doing his work in normal conditions, after having made an effort to join the Army, is no less patriotic than the man in uniform.

CHAPTER 4

WOMEN'S SUFFRAGE

The story by Sir Arthur Conan Doyle serves to illustrate two significant aspects of the First World War that lay ahead of Britain in the summer of 1914. The first, that it was to be conducted on a geographical scale unknown in past years; the second, that it would involve not only the fighting men, but also those left behind, and the women and children. Women were no strangers to the 'front line', but had previously been attendees, rather than active participants. True, they had fulfilled a nursing role, but because they were on-site, not because they had travelled for that express purpose.

The third aspect of waging war would be the lack of any chivalry shown by either side. The siege of Britain, and the use of starvation, was an aspect of war which some could not countenance. As Conan Doyle says in replying to his critics, the story is of what might happen, not what will happen. It is a story which should serve to warn or caution the reader, not to offer any certainty of events still to come. As Conan Doyle warns, Britain is in danger of being caught napping if the threat is ignored or thought too preposterous. Thousands of women were to be caught napping in the battle for women's suffrage. They were to be outflanked by happenstance, not by strategy.

It's interesting that Conan Doyle, speaking though Captain John Sirius, advocated one of the prime tenets of fascism, that of protectionism and the use of tariffs to protect the home market. That is not to say that Conan Doyle was a fascist, but he did realise that such fears and solutions were already in general circulation before the First World War brought them into focus. Fears such as these were shared by many ordinary people in the country. Some offered simple ineffective solutions, others ignored the problem in order to enjoy the cheap bounty from the Empire, a few offered a more radical and unacceptable solution, which was to take the law into their own hands.

In the fight for women's suffrage, the democratic process had failed the suffragettes. They were forced by circumstances to take direct action against those who were unwilling to share power, forced to act against the law of the land to get a fair hearing. Their protests were heard by the men in charge, but they were not heeded. Their crimes were born out of frustration, out of feeling powerless to persuade those who retained power over them, and out of a desperation to be heard.

On the outbreak of war the entire fabric of their fight was snatched from beneath them. Emmeline Pankhurst withdrew her support in favour of propping up the government, without consulting those young women on the front line of the fight. Whether it was the right decision for the situation, or the right one for the country, thousands of women had the decision taken out of their hands only to be presented with a course of action that was not of their choice. Again the 'establishment' had dictated how the population should think – again the wealthy and influential had dominated.

As writers Conan Doyle and Rudyard Kipling foretold, the need for volunteers to join the army became paramount. Encouraging young men to join the army became the new face of patriotism and one to which the disenfranchised suffragettes rallied. When Charles Penrose-Fitzgerald called for them to become the conscience of Britain's manhood, they answered the call for, after all, their argument had been with the governance of men, not the governance of kings. So, from that call was born the White Feather Brigade, not an organisation, but a cause to be pursued. Had it been adopted by wiser heads it may not have made such crass mistakes as it did, may not have used scatter-gun tactics rather than targeting its prey, may not have attracted such ill will. The idea, while sound in principle, needed to be managed, rather than be left in the hands of impressionable young women. Having stirred up a hornet's nest, Penrose-Fitzgerald appears to have walked away.

By the end of 1915 it was clear that the attempts of the White Feather Brigade had failed to raise adequate volunteers, and so conscription was introduced by the government. The suffragettes, with no leader and lately obsessed with donating white feathers, had failed again to achieve their goals. By the time that conscription was introduced they were no longer suffragettes, there was no longer an effective WSPU to lead them. The greater good had taken precedence over the interests of the individual women at the 'coal face' – another tenet.

With conscription came the concept of conscientious objection and with that the possibility of identifying real 'shirkers'. The White Feather Brigade regained a little of what had been lost through bad, or no, management, but attracted criticism of their own war efforts, which were found to be wanting. Although the methods employed were met with opposition, the basic principles behind their movement were not. When the White Feather Brigade was first introduced it was met with almost universal approval, only incurring criticism of the methods employed.

But suppose that Emmeline Pankhurst, and the leadership of the WSPU, had not abandoned the rank and file of the women's suffrage movement. The government might have simply rolled over and given them the vote – perhaps. The prevailing argument was that the government ought not to be distracted by something so inconsequential, at a time when other events were so critical. But votes for women was not an inconsequential issue to thousands of women up and down the country, and perhaps choosing that time to insist would have been the sensible thing to do – the suffragettes were not consulted.

An alternative course of action would have been for the Pankhursts to have taken the bestowing of white feathers under the wing of the WSPU. This would have achieved the same ends with regard to support for the government, but would have maintained the WSPU, and their primary cause, at the forefront of the political agenda. Thousands of young women, whether they were with the Red Cross, working in factories or at home aiding the recruiting drive, would not have felt so abandoned and left to plough their own furrow.

Who can say if women's suffrage would have come about during or shortly after the war. As it happened, it took ten years from the end of the war for men and women to gain the same voting rights. In that time, young women coming back from front line service were not greatly lauded, those who had worked in the factories had lost their jobs, and those who had done their bit in boosting recruitment had been criticised and ridiculed. By 1928, when women's suffrage was finally granted, another outlet for their energy was on offer.

> Comrades, it is the eve of our parting. Those of us who have had the longest sentences to serve have seen many a farewell waved up towards our cell windows from the great prison gate as time after time it opened for release. The jail yard, too, where we exercise, now seems spacious, though at first it was thronged with our fellow prisoners. Yet not one of them has really left us. Whenever in through we re-enter that yard, within its high, grim walls we see each as we knew her there: our revered Leader, Mrs. Pankhurst, courageous, serene, smiling; Dr Ethel Smyth, joyous and terrific, whirling through a game of rounders with as much intentness as if she were conducting a symphony; Dr L. Garrett Anderson, in whose eyes gaiety and gravity are never far apart – but we cannot name them all, for there are scores who made that yard a pleasant place.

With the ever-growing feelings of emancipation in the air, with women taking a more active part in post-war Britain, this maverick generation of young women were denied a formal role in running the country. They had been released from the moral straitjacket of the Edwardian era, fashions were beginning to feel free and easy and personal romantic preferences were beginning to dominate. Within a few years of the war ending, Britain would be entering the age of the 'flapper'. Young women of the 1920s would become part of the political movement for reform; if denied access to the ballot box, they would take to the streets in order to raise their voices and be heard.

By 1920, women had gained the vote in parts of the Dominions, many of the states in America and most of Scandinavia; even in Germany. A man returning from war might have been disappointed by the reality of finding his 'land fit for heroes', women equally so, but it was not *her* land, but *his* land. Where they had once looked to the WSPU for female leadership, they now sought female leadership from other, more unconventional directions.

In parallel with the changing political developments was the breakdown of conditions in Ireland. Much to the disgust of the ultra-conservatives, there was an on-going guerrilla war in progress over the Irish fight for independence. The Royal Irish Constabulary were supplemented by temporary constables known colloquially as the Black and Tans, recruited from the ranks of ex-soldiers who then employed brutal methods to control the local population. The introduction of martial law in some parts of Ireland was anathema to many in the London drawing rooms. It was the issue of the Black and Tans that prompted Oswald Moseley's departure from the Conservative Party.

> Who's for the game, the biggest that's played,
> The red crashing game of a fight?
> Who'll grip and tackle the job unafraid?
> And who thinks he'd rather sit tight?

Who'll toe the line for the signal to "Go!"?
Who'll give his country a hand?
Who wants a turn to himself in the show?
And who wants a seat in the stand?
Who knows it won't be a picnic – not much-
Yet eagerly shoulders a gun?
Who would much rather come back with a crutch
Than lie low and be out of the fun?
Come along, lads –
But you'll come on all right –
For there's only one course to pursue,
Your country is up to her neck in a fight,
And she's looking and calling for you.

CHAPTER 5

THE BRITISH FASCISTI

Rotha Lintorn-Orman had been born Rotha Orman in 1895; the name Lintorn had been added in tribute to her maternal grandfather Field-Marshal John Lintorn Arabin Simmons. Her father, John Orman, also came from a military family who served in India and then returned to Britain when Rotha's paternal grandfather was killed while on tour as a local magistrate. Rotha, from a very young age, was engulfed in a culture that embraced and held Britain and its Empire close to its heart.

As a 19-year-old, Rotha had first joined the Women's Reserve Ambulance Corps (WRAC) in London, who were charged with the task of helping soldiers, coming home from France, find their way across London. Her tasks involved driving injured soldiers from Victoria Station to other London stations by ambulance. During her period of service she was actively involved in rescuing survivors of the first bombing of London from Zeppelins. The members of the WRAC wore a distinctive uniform, perhaps a comfortable reflection of her days in the Girl Guides, the first of many to come.

Rotha's mother, Blanch, had the strongest influence on the young woman who had then left her home shores in the early years of the war, to serve with the Scottish Women's Hospital in Serbia. While she was away, driving an ambulance on the front line, she developed a liking for manly dress and demeanour, and a liking for sexual partners of the same gender. This could have been her basic nature coming to the fore, but the environment she was living in was one that made the culture of the women with whom she worked seem perfectly normal.

Many of the women who enlisted with these non-governmental agencies had been suffragettes before the war, adventurous young women who were used to living on the edge, risking their life and liberty; before the war with the British police and during the war with Ottoman soldiers. Now returned to civilian life, they were without a cause to fight for and living the life that had been planned for them in some previous existence by their parents. These, of course, were the upper-class girls – the working classes were busy working, marrying and child-bearing.

Blanch's drawing room would see the coming together of men and women from the upper class, who believed they were witnessing the passing of a way of life that they had enjoyed and depended on their whole life. For them the threat of socialism presented a very real danger, one that threatened their standing in society. Senior military families were generally seen as loyal and patriotic, superficially as models of British society, and their status never questioned. That status was under threat and they, and other groups like them, needed to take action in defence of that status.

Blanch Lintorn-Orman was 63 years old in 1922, and hadn't the energy to lead the fight against socialism alone, but she did have the means to finance it. She had a 27-year-old daughter who had fire in her belly and the sheer audacity to take on the world and win. A young woman who had chosen a lifestyle that was at odds with established society, that flew in the face of convention and that would appeal to those who were ready to be called to a radical form of political action. Blanch's husband was not part of her drawing room politics and, although not formally separated, appeared to lead a life completely devoid of politics – and away from Blanch.

Rotha was not living in London with her parents, but at Lower Langford Manor in Somerset, the country home of the Simmons family, now passed down to Blanch Lintorn-Orman. Here Rotha lived the life of a 'gentleman farmer', working in the fields but also following the pursuits of the idle rich. She was said to entertain many like-minded young women for weekend parties, all of similarly unconventional habits. Blanch, concerned that Rotha should find a purpose in life, saw her as the nominal political leader that her drawing room committee were looking for. She also realised that such an adventure was to cost her dear and that it would mean the investment of her fortune in the political ambitions of a dying breed.

Rotha's own political views were one-dimensional. Concerned about the rise of socialism, one place in Europe where there were signs of opposition to the steady march toward communism was in Italy, with Benito Mussolini at its head. Rotha and her mother felt that the two major tenets of the movement embodied what was needed in British political life; the sacrifice of the individual's self-interest to those of the country's, and the enforcement of those rules by a single strong leader – Mussolini. The threatened coup in Italy came about without the workers' threatened march on Rome, success being brought about by threat and propaganda, and was finally the result of a legitimate, if unusual, transfer of power.

In Britain, there was no obvious equivalent of Mussolini, and the working class could not be relied upon to throw up such an individual from within their ranks, someone who through sheer personality could persuade others of their worth and their vision – a leader. Mussolini had been a socialist politician and journalist, but his socialist views had morphed into a more demanding form, one where his followers awarded him Godlike qualities. Britain's socialists had only just begun to gain a foothold in the political process and were fighting hard to survive in a hitherto two-party system.

In truth, fascism grew out of socialist ideals, looking after the interests of the workers, ensuring that the fruits of the native population's efforts were rewarded, rather than be underpriced in the face of foreign competition. Internationalism was the enemy, socialism being the root problem. According to Mussolini's theory, international socialism prevented the imposition of tariffs to protect home producers; without tariffs there could be no protection from world price fluctuations – the country with the lowest labour costs would always win.

Popular culture tells the story of how Rotha Lintorn-Orman, while tending to her garden in deepest Somerset, experienced a 'Road to Damascus' moment. She realised that Britain needed such a movement to counteract the growing move towards socialism and internationalism. She would take as her model the movement created by Mussolini in Italy, the notion of the individual's interests being subservient to that of the state and the workers rising in defence of patriotism. She would even take the name that Mussolini used, but make it a British version of an Italian concept – the British Fascisti (BF).

One leading member of Blanch's circle was Alan Ian Percy, the 8th Duke of Northumberland, who was an extremely vocal member and owned the Boswell Printing and Publishing Company which published *The Patriot* to air his very right-wing views. It was decided that this publication would be ideal to garner support for Rotha's ideas, and so a series of advertisements was published in *The Patriot* and the call from Rotha was answered. Some notable names were included, among them members of the Conservative Party, who saw no conflict in them being a member of both. The aim, after all, was to support the current government, not to overthrow it.

The BF formed, control was placed in the hands of a Grand Council in which Rotha played only a minor part. The president was Lord Garvagh, who is credited as joint founder with Rotha, and the other members of the council were made up of an unusual number of generals and admirals. At this early stage Rotha is being written out of the narrative of the BF and is fulfilling only a figurehead role, secured by her mother's financial support. She headed up the women's division, which amounted to two main responsibilities; the first to ensure that the fascist message was well represented in the local Sunday schools, and the second to help steward meetings and to eject female protesters.

Rotha was well suited to this stewarding role. Her time overseas with the SWH had given her a taste for the physical side of life, dressing as a man, through necessity and comfort, and adopting a manly image and manner of speaking. She had retained this style while living on the farm in Somerset and had drawn around her a squadron of similarly minded young women for weekend parties. It can be said with little doubt that Rotha was not one of the young ladies destined to be presented at court as a debutante, but neither can it be said that she was destined to become a charismatic political leader in the mould of Mussolini in Italy, or Lenin in Russia.

It is doubtful whether the membership of the BF ever really embraced the full fascist doctrine, as developed in Italy, being regarded more as an ultra-conservative, pro-empire, pressure group. The BF membership, while pronouncing the danger of Jewish financiers plotting with Bolsheviks, did not advance any anti-Semitic sentiment. That is not to say that individual members did not hold any anti-Semitic views, but it was no part of Rotha Lintorn-Orman's call for support. In fact one member, Arnold Leese, would later found a party of his own in which such views could come to the fore.

More moderate in her views was another of the early members, Viscountess Downe, born Dorothy Ffolkes at Hillington Hall, near King's Lynn in Norfolk. During the war she had handed over Hillington Hall to be used as a Royal Flying Corps convalescence home. The Downe family had already allocated their Yorkshire home to the Royal Flying Corps, and this was a further sign of her deep-seated patriotism. She had, in her younger days, been one of the Queen's ladies in waiting and, being a close neighbour to the royal family at Sandringham, had remained a lifelong friend. She was also the Chair of the local Conservative Women's Association, and felt no conflict of interest in belonging to both.

> . . . newly-formed organisation called the British Fascisti, which has Lord Garvagh for president,. and a woman secretary who signs herself 'R L Lintorn-Orman, Adjutant-General and Secretary to the Council' . . . a tall and muscular young woman . . . There are women as well as men in the movement . . . When on duty the Fascisti wear armlets and have a button badge bearing the letter 'F' and have the words For king and Country, "We are out to get Britain exclusively for the British, and will ensure free speech even if we have to meet force with force."

Within a year, Lord Garvagh, otherwise Leopold Ernest Stratford George Canning, had resigned as president, citing his home in Ireland as being too far from London to be truly effective. He was replaced by another of the early members, Brigadier R.B.D. Blakeney, who came from a military background and who could be said to continue under an ultra-conservative rather than a true fascist doctrine. He was of the opinion that Mussolini's model of fascism could never work in Britain, likening the BF more to overgrown boy scouts than to true fascists.

His derogatory reference to the boy scouts may have been a direct slight to Rotha Lintorn-Orman, the founder. She and Blakeney were not easy bedfellows within the BF and her association with the founding of the boy scouts, then the girl scouts and later the girl guides, offered him something child-like with which to label her. Everything else she had done since then was immaterial in Blakeney's eyes; her service during the war, both in Britain and Serbia, and her work with the Red Cross, after being invalided home with malaria, cut very little ice with such a man.

Blakeney's first priority was to change the BF structure from that of a boy scouts committee into a more disciplined and military style of organisation. The second was to change the Italian sounding name to one that would attract the support of their fellow countrymen. It was to be renamed the British Fascists (BF). At the same time Blakeney reached out to the Anti-Socialist Union, a group that pre-dated the BF by twenty-five years, and which held some very advanced and sophisticated views which, today, would be considered a modern take on socialism.

His approaches came to nothing. At this stage in the fight against socialism there was a clear lack of a consensus among the far right in politics. That space was made up of small groups, even individuals, each occupying a small niche and attracting its own supporters. With no coordinated philosophy to rally around, each group possessed the capacity to split in two over the most minor difference. With no central leadership, there was no strong individual to try to heal the rifts that had developed, and no central management structure to calm the pomposity of individuals whose personal egos were put before the overall good of the organisation.

Having made these changes, Blakeney himself was faced with a split in the British Fascists. Led initially by L.A. Howard, and then by Lieutenant Colonel Henry Rippon-Seymour, the splinter group attempted to pursue a more definite path towards establishing a fascist state. This new group, which called themselves the National Fascisti, attempted to follow the Italian model more closely by calling for, as Mussolini had done, a panel of experts to make major decisions, rather than such things being entrusted to elected representatives. They also included a call for racial purity in Britain, introducing antisemitism into their meetings.

In imitation of Mussolini's fascists, members wore black shirts and received some limited military training. Constantly seeking publicity, they would enter into events likely to provide headlines for the newspapers. One such publicity stunt was to highjack a lorry carrying copies of the *Daily Herald*, and then deliberately crash it. Emulating events in Italy, the National Fascisti engaged in pitched battles with communists at their outdoor meetings and rallies, significant in that it introduced the pseudo-military style behaviour into the British version of fascism and gave full rein to Arnold Leese and William Joyce, both of whom were to became notorious in later years.

Later, changing its name to the British National Fascisti, the group introduced boxing and fencing clubs for its members, reinforcing the physical nature of their approach to politics. The group was shortlived, however. Rippon-Seymour, who was very fond of waving an unsheathed sword in the face of opponents, was finally accused of threatening their Croydon branch leader with a sword and gun. In return the Croydon leader, Charles Eyres, confronted Rippon-Seymour with his gang of club- and baton-wielding supporters. Rippon-Seymour was eventually convicted for that offence at the Old Bailey.

The conviction did nothing for the reputation of the individuals concerned, nor for the right-wing activists involved. The spat was found, by the police, to concern the finances of the British National Fascisti. The nature of these accusations was not the subject of any prosecution, but it was sufficient to reinforce the notion that fascists, no matter from which group, were a bunch of thugs – at best unconventional, else criminal and beyond deserving of trust. The matter induced a fear among the supporters, if not the members themselves, about their association with men who would bring the party into such disrepute, and who may be hiding darker secrets behind their middle-class veil.

> At a meeting of British National Fascisti, in Hyde Park yesterday, the platform was rushed and the speaker cut on the face with the broken flagstaff of a Union Jack. Mr. Howe was speaking when a section of the crowd made a rush forward. Friends of Mr. Howe struggled against the attackers, and the latter beat a retreat when policemen appeared. The platform and flag were re-erected, and Mr. Howe went on with his speech.

One member whom some might regard as noteworthy was Lillias Irma Valerie Arkell-Smith, born Barker who, after being married and separated, and then living with another man and again separated, reverted to living in the guise of a man, under the name Sir Victor Barker. She then, as a man, entered into a marriage with one Elfrida Emma Haward. Joining the British National Fascisti, it was he (or she) that owned the un-licenced gun that was wielded by Henry Rippon-Seymour. He and Valerie Arkell-Smith left the British National Fascisti shortly following this.

Political unrest began to grow in Britain with the coal miners being faced with a longer working day and their wages being cut. They began industrial action, but the Trades Union Congress got behind them and organised many other trades unions to join them on the picket lines. This was viewed as a revolution of sorts, but not a coup, rather as a challenge to the established order – precisely as Blanch Lintorn-Orman and her drawing room committee of 1923 had feared. It presented the first steps of organised socialism, marching towards its goal of forcing Russian-style communism upon Britain.

From the point of view of the coal mine owners, the bottom had fallen out of the market for a number of reasons, none of which were due directly to them. During the war there had been an unprecedented demand for coal from industry, and their best seams had been worked out to meet the demand. During the war it had been difficult to export coal, even if they could have found the capacity, and this had allowed other countries, particularly America, to take that market. In 1925 the 'gold standard' had been re-introduced, which made the value of sterling too high to secure an effective export market with a bulk commodity like coal.

The final blow came with the implementation of the Dawes Plan, an American scheme whereby Germany, forced to pay reparation to France and Italy in a traded currency, was permitted to do so by means of coal instead. This was tantamount to providing those two countries with free coal, with the consequence of denying those export markets to British coal mine owners. The government offered the mine owners a nine-month subsidy to avoid the wage cut while the Samuel Commission reported back. When they did report, they still recommended a reduction in wages and a withdrawal of the mine owners' subsidy.

> The German Budget for 1924-25 has shown a safe balance, and has in fact, yielded a surplus of receipts over expenditure, and Germany has also succeeded in providing and maintaining a stable currency.

Despite last-minute efforts to negotiate, the General Strike was set to begin at one minute before midnight on Monday, 3 May 1926. Even the Labour Party was anxious as to the outcome of the strike, in view of their knowledge that there were some amongst the strikers who planned the feared revolution, a fear that was articulated by the right-wing fascist groups. Being relatively fresh on the scene, the Labour Party's great fear was that with talk of revolution it may lose electoral support in the country, through alienating workers outside the militant coal miners, railwaymen, transport workers, printers, dockers, ironworkers, steelworkers and seamen, and that the strikers may therefore be limited to only those industries.

The government had benefitted by being aware for some months that the strike was coming. During that time they had been able to plan on what tactics they were able to employ in order to mitigate the worst effects. Plans were in place to bolster the number of staff at crucial centres such as ports, plus the introduction of employers' representatives to ensure that shipments were progressed with minimum delay. Haulage was protected to some extent by the government establishing private contracts with the use of volunteers to load and drive. By the February of 1926, the home secretary was able to tell the Cabinet that matters were in hand and that little was left to be done.

In contrast, the unions made little, or no, preparation for the strike. In part this was due to fear of losing control to the militant element, in part to a lack of control from the TUC and in part to the belief that the union arguments alone were sufficient for them to win the day, and that any planned pro-active plans could be interpreted as preparation for a revolution. Ernest Bevin, speaking after the strike, said:

> With regard to the preparation for the strike, there was no preparation until April 27, and I do not want anyone to go away from this conference under the impression that the General Council had any particular plan to run the movement. In fact the General Council did not sit down to draft the plans until they were called together on April 27, and it is better for everybody to know the task was thrown upon us from April 27 to May 1, and when that task is understood you will be able to appreciate not the little difficulties but the wonderful response and organisation we had.

The impending General Strike promised a crisis whereby the right wing of politics, including the various fascist groups, would have a chance to test their mettle and 'save' the British Empire and all it stood for. The two dominant fascist groups had looked forward to this situation since their formation, prophesying that the socialists would eventually begin the revolution and that it would mark the rising of the working class. The BFs, despite their name, were essentially conservatives and seeking to support the status quo, as might the police, which meant supporting the government; the British National Fascisti were similarly motivated, but acted as if martial law were already imposed.

Both fascist groups were under the illusion that they held a more significant position in the public eye than was the case. In actual fact, the two fascist groups accounted for only a tiny minority of those who volunteered to assist the Conservative government in its time of need. Most came from the middle classes, from the universities and from the non-working ladies of leisure who answered the call to defend the empire. The anticipated coup threatened their place in society – there would be no place for them if the Bolsheviks took over.

While preparations were being made to prepare for the General Strike, a young man was looking for a parliamentary seat. He had previously sat as a Conservative but had 'crossed the floor' to sit as an independent, and had since joined the Labour Party. His wife was an active member of the party, and both would eventually become Labour MPs. Oswald and Cynthia Mosley would become the antithesis of Rotha Lintorn-Orman and her drawing room BFs, seeking to belittle her at every opportunity.

> Mr. Oswald Mosley, talented young member Labour-socialist party, and his wife. Lady Cynthia Mosley, appear to be more amused than anything else over the public challenge of Mr. Mosley's father, Sir Oswald Mosley, which appeared in the Press yesterday morning. The father challenged his Socialist son and daughter-in-law, instead of talking about titles, to do something more tangible, and renounce a considerable portion of their wealth to their less fortunate fellow-socialists.

This conflict between the poor and the rich socialist was one of the factors which divided them. Whereas the poor saw the redistribution of wealth as fundamental to solving their real-life problems, the rich viewed it as theoretical bandage, a salve or balm, with which to illustrate a social lecture. Similarly, the poor socialist, while committed to taking a share of his rich brother's wealth, was less enthusiastic in sharing his own with the destitute.

The fundamental attraction was that within the fascist structure there seemed an opportunity to construct a society that raised living standards for everybody. There would still be rich and poor, but the differences would less, and the cream would still rise to the surface. This was nonsense of course, but the disappointment of not having returned to a land fit for heroes, and the anticipation of a General Strike, was a powerful reason to look for a utopian future.

CHAPTER 6

THE GENERAL STRIKE

As part of the government's plans to mitigate the effects of the General Strike, the concept of volunteers coming to their aid was high on the agenda. There was no shortage of volunteers to step forward, but using them to the best advantage required some organisation. Many of the middle class, mostly women, saw it as an opportunity to take part in an unusual social event, one that they could recount at every soiree they attended. It also presented them with an opportunity to be photographed in working garb while being recruited by the likes of Lady Astor, a Conservative Member of Parliament. An amateur poem was published in one of the provincial newspapers; two verses are reproduced below.

The Middle Class do not go on strike, the Peace to jeopardize;
The land of their birth they don't blackmail with "Stand and deliver !" nor rant and rail,.
And they do not Bolshevise.
When the agitators howl and rave much blather and little tact.
They say: "It's all very well, my son, but mile of theory, thinly spun, is not worth an inch fact!

The Middle Class have a right to live as well the right pay;

Two parties only in strikes, absurd! Permit me to indicate third;
And we mean to have our say.
You cut off supplies of coal, or milk or gas, and protests you spurn.
But there is proverb to this effect, And you will know it, I expect:

That even the worm will turn!

It came as a disappointment to the BF, and to the British National Fascisti, that they were not to ride to the defence of their king and country under the banner of fascism. Up until the last minute the two groups had seen themselves as all that stood between the government and the threat of rampant socialism or communism, only for their offers of help to be spurned in favour of a more measured and cautious approach; not a head-on conflict, but a politically sensitive solution that did not prevent further discussion.

The government, rather than enter into direct conflict with the Trades Union Council, chose to act through a voluntary third party, the Organisation for the Maintenance of Supply (OMS), under the leadership of Lord Hardinge. Such an organisation, while being welcomed by some newspapers, was harshly critisised by others for being aligned with the Fascists. In an attempt to reassure the doubters, Lord Jellicoe and other top military men joined Lord Hardinge, and also brought some military discipline to the proceedings.

The announcement of the OMS was enthusiastically greeted by the *Daily Mail*, and other right-wing newspapers. It was met with disdain by socialists, likening it to a fascist organisation, a view shared by some other conservative publications, comparing it with the American fascist-like organisation, Ku Klux Klan. To be fair to the OMS, there was no hint of racial prejudice in any of their activities during the General Strike. The banning of the word 'fascist' demonstrated, at least, its intent.

First among those groups to volunteer were the BF and the British National Fascisti, both looking forward to the opportunity to flex their political and physical muscles. A worrying factor was the association of the word fascism with the threat of physical violence. Rotha Lintorn-Orman was associated with groups of 'stewards' keeping order at BF meetings, and Henry Rippon-Seymour was known for his erratic personal behaviour leading to his arrest and imprisonment.

Both made their approaches to the OMS, and both met the same rebuff. While either had the word 'fascist' in their name, there was no way in which they could operate under the OMS umbrella. Hardinge was adamant that his organisation was, and would continue to be, independent of political bias.

> The Society seeks to enrol immediately volunteers who would, in the event of an emergency arising loyally keep the promise now made, and turn out to assist the authorities to keep the supplies and essential services running. Five classes are required : (a) Protection; (b) maintaining public services; (c) transport driver; (d) messenger (motor cyclist, etc.); (e) members who promise to support and contribute.

Of course it was not independent. An organisation set up specifically to mitigate the effects of the General Strike, to provide what some might refer to as 'scab labour' and to deliberately break the union picket lines, is displaying its fundamental purpose – to enter the General Strike on the side of the government and the employers. When the OMS received government support, and then operated under government control, it reinforced the notion that it was, in reality, acting as an arm of government. To the working classes it represented the enemy, as one newspaper letter writer suggested.

> I have received and declined an invitation to become a member of the above organisation (*Organisation for the Maintenance of Supply*). It is clearly the duty of the government of the day to protect the public interest in case of need, and if it fails to do so, it is not likely that an organisation, consisting, apparently, of members of one political party is going to be more successful. If the present government is so feeble that it cannot act with promptitude and decision in a time of crisis, the sooner it is got rid of the better. As a matter of fact, I believe that the risk of events developing in the manner suggested by the promoters of the O.M.S. is greatly exaggerated. However that may be, and without questioning their motives, I am of the opinion that the setting up of the O.M.S. is likely to prove a hindrance to those of us who are doing our best to promote a better spirit in industry.

While the British National Fascisti rejected the suggestion of a name change outright, the BF was split on the issue. Rotha Lintorn-Orman was firmly against rejecting the association with fascism, while Brigadier Blakeney was of the opinion that to be part of the OMS was to the long-term benefit of the anti-socialist campaign. Although he carried much of the BF with him, Rotha as founder, along with her mother's money, carried the day.

Blakeney, and his followers, did relinquish the name fascist, and grouped together under a new name, that of the Loyalists. He took with him Patrick James Boyle, the 8th Earl of Glasgow, and Lord Ernest William Hamilton, both Conservative supporters; they followed Blakeney in wanting to support the government in countering the General Strike and considered that the dropping of the fascist name was of less importance. Viscountess Downe stayed behind with Rotha Lintorn-Orman and the BF.

> Brigadier-General R.B.D. Blakeney, president of the British Fascists, and Admiral Armstrong, Lord Ernest Hamilton, Sir lames Hewatt, Major Battine and Mr. Frank Sale, members of the council, have resigned following a division of opinion on a question of policy. The dissenters will immediately form a new patriotic association, The Loyalists, which will be organised on a civil and not military basis. General Blakeney told the *Daily News* last night that when the British Fascists offered their services to the government they were told that, as long as they were a semi-military organisation, they could not be employed on work of State. "A great many of our members are in favour of reorganisation on the lines of the O.M.S" he said, "and are anxious to be of any assistance in a crisis. "We are, therefore, hoping to form a strong civil body, which will be in an alliance of patriotic bodies, composed of members, all of whom are willing to work."

With the departure of Blakeney, the control of the BF reverted to Rotha and her mother's drawing room committee, boy scouts or not; from then on Blakeney almost disappeared from sight, submerged beneath the behemoth which was the OMS. The two fascist groups, BF and the British National Fascisti, each played their part in resisting the strike, not by standing in for those who withheld their labour, but by ensuring that those who resisted the strike could hold their meetings without hinderance, and ensuring that those supporting the strike should feel unsafe in pronouncing their views in public.

Over the weekend, running up to the start of the strike, negotiations became more fraught than they had been previously. The government's rhetoric became more intransigent, that of the Trades Union Council more stoic. Baldwin maintained that the impending General Strike threatened the very freedom of Britain's constitution,

Churchill that the Labour Party wanted to overthrow the government. Ramsey MacDonald claimed the moral high ground by insisting that the unions sincerely wished for a settlement, and criticised the intransigence of the government.

In Hyde Park, two communists and three members of the BF engaged in a day-long running battle, which culminated in a large crowd attempting to intervene on the side of the communists. The police had finally to rescue the situation with raised batons, and bring in mounted men who eventually cleared the streets. Such skirmishes were fairly common during the duration of the General Strike, individual members from either side of the red/black divide taking on the role of hooligan and revelling in street violence.

During the General Strike, although the fascist groups played their part, they constituted a very small influence in the event. The main conflict would be largely confined to that between the strikers and the middle-class volunteers, organised by the OMS, and most readily seen in central London, where transport links would be heavily affected. With commuter links from the suburbs suspended, and intra-London bus routes not working effectively, the loss of working days in the city was to be catastrophic, with damage to London's reputation abroad.

At the regional offices of the OMS, located outside London, they did not reject help from the fascists quite so readily. In many parts of the country the fascists drove lorries and buses, distributed news sheets, delivered coal and distributed food. There was not the middle-class army of volunteers waiting to be photographed whilst serving tea to the strike breakers as there were in London. Outside London the strike breakers lived cheek by jowl with those on strike – life was lived a little more sensitively in the provinces.

On the Tuesday morning, the first morning of the strike, there was little evidence of the conflict anticipated. Buses and trains were noticeable by their absence, and the streets were choked with people walking to work in the hopes that life would be continuing as normal. In London, it seemed that every private car was on the road, resulting in gridlock and, as a consequence, many were abandoned, leading to yet more congestion. In the middle of this mayhem the government was keen to insist that the OMS was ensuring that food supplies were unaffected.

At some 'pinch points' on the road network, such as the Blackwall Tunnel, strikers stopped cars and forced their occupants to abandon the vehicle and continue their journey on foot. The police were forced to act and made repeated baton charges to restore order. With the printers on strike, there were only a few, limited-page newspapers in circulation. With limited newsprint reserves in the country, the government ordered supplies from The Netherlands, and commandeered papermaking and storage facilities in Britain so that pro-government information could continue to be distributed.

There was pressure on the Trades Union Council to produce its own newspaper during the strike to counter that which was already being printed and distributed by the British National Fascisti. In the first edition, the Fascists produced a particularly racist attack on Shapurji Saklatvala, communist MP for Battersea, and of Indian origin, claiming that Battersea was being taken over by the Bolsheviks. In an open letter, the president wrote.

> You are supposed to be an "Honourable" Member of the House of Commons, a place you should consider it an honour to enter, but apparently you do not. In that House you have recently made a speech full of what the true Briton – whatever his faults may be – Winston Churchill has termed "terminological inexactitudes", but what the "man in the street" plainly call LIES . . . The too large number of "coloured persons" like yourself brought from a condition of filth, slavery and savagery and ignorance by the efforts of a brave and loyal handful of Britons who do possess "traditional sentiments" and have been suborned and seduced from a rightful loyalty to Britain

> by such glib-tongued sedition mongers as you . . . know full well that you are but an Adventurer, sitting on the Raft of Opportunity, afloat on the Sea of Communism awaiting the Wind of Revolution.

The British National Fascisti had introduced racial hatred into their campaign, a step which Rotha Lintorn-Orman and her BF had not wanted. Following that publication, the *British Gazette*, produced by the government, and the *British Worker*, produced by the Trades Union Council, entered into a war of words, each to boost their own supporters; neither to reach out to the other side. Both publications concentrated on the propaganda of conflict, the steadfastness of the government on the one hand and the stoicism of the workers on the other.

A major criticism of either newspaper was that it directed itself at too narrow a readership. Neither was aimed at a readership that held views opposite to those of the editorial team. Each was preaching to the converted, so neither was able to influence opinion, they were able only to reinforce opinions already held. The technique was simply to regurgitate propaganda from the press office of either the government or the Trades Union Council – both so obviously the views of committees.

Both fascist groups were engaged in the protection of individuals and property, rather than in driving lorries or trains carrying vital supplies. They saw themselves as being there to protect the volunteers who were working under the direction of the OMS. In many ways this was a role more suited to their talents than would have been the case should they have been otherwise employed. These mobile groups, ferried from place to place by lorry, were brutal in their task of putting down any resistance. These 'Q' Divisions included in their number groups of fascist women, to deal with female opposition, thus avoiding claims of male bullying.

The London docks, brought to a standstill by strike action, were unable to distribute imported foodstuffs, and so the government amassed soldiers and armoured cars in the area around Hyde Park in the West End. Finally they set off for the docks and, fully loaded, set off back to Hyde Park, ready for a second run. The government through the OMS was in control, and was effectively beating the strike without the aid of the fascists, who were making very little impact on the outcome of the dispute, except at the propaganda level.

However the Trades Union Council was of the opinion that their lives were in danger from the government should they lose the fight. One MP believed they would be taken into custody for their own protection, where they would be shot. Not by the police or army, but by those 'damned fascists'. He said 'the money is not in the industry, so the strike is against the state, Churchill is the man who will play the big part in this'. There are echoes here of an Italian-style fascist revolution, rather than communist agitators within the unions.

The government, rather than try to break the strike by force alone, turned to the law in order to establish some way in which the unions could be found to be acting outside their legal remit. They gambled on the individual unions being vulnerable should they be denied their war-chest and that war-chest being held in financial institutions, under conservative-minded directors, with no chance of the banks denying the government access. Individual unions would then have a long-drawn-out, and expensive, fight to recover their funds.

The High Court finally ruled that, although the strike within the coal industry was quite legal, other industries coming out in support of them was not. This meant that there was a real danger that the funds of other unions might be sequestered and further restrictions imposed.

> The resent declaration of Sir John Simon as to the illegality of the general strike received the support of a decision in the High Court yesterday. This was contained in a judgement delivered by Mr. Justice Astbury in reference to an application made by the executive of the Sailor's and Fireman's Union, for an injunction to

> restrain the secretary of one of the branches of the union from calling out members of the union from their work without the authority of the executive, who are taking a ballot of the members on the question whether they are willing to withdraw their labour in response to the call of the T.U.C. Mr. Justice Lawrence last week granted interim injunctions against the district secretary of the union in the Mersey area. and two executives of the Liverpool branch, and by consent these were yesterday made perpetual.

This was too much for the Trades Union Council to allow to develop into a direct dispute between the unions and the government, with the courts and the government being on the same side. The volunteers stayed in place, in case there should be any resistance to the strike being called off, but there was no turning back and the strike was ended with a whimper rather than a bang.

King George V issued a message to the people in an attempt to heal the rifts. This was what the fascists wanted to hear, although with a slightly more triumphal tone, considering that a revolution had been averted. After all, the king had not been imprisoned in Windsor Castle, the extended royal family had not been murdered and the government had not been the subject of a Bolshevik coup. The country was quiet, the institutions still functioning; Ascot, Wimbledon, Henley and the cricket tests against Australia took place. Of more interest to the working class, Bolton Wanderers won the Cup Final, and Hull Kingston Rovers were the Rugby League champions.

> The nation has just passed through a period of extreme anxiety. It was today announced that the General Strike had been brought to an end. At such moment it is supremely important to bring together all my people to confront the difficult situation which still remains.

> This task requires the co-operation of all able and well-disposed men in the country. Even with such help it will be difficult, but it will not be impossible. Let us forget what elements of bitterness the last few days may have created, only remembering how steady and how orderly the country has remained, though severely tested, and forthwith address ourselves to the task of bringing in to being a peace which will be lasting because, forgetting the past, it looks only to the future with the hopefulness of a united people.

The dispute between coal miners and the coal mine owners continued for some months. Many attempts to reconcile the two sides were made, none of them successful. With the strike broken there was not the impetus to fight. The coal mine owners maintained the upper hand and with union funds nearly exhausted, and the mine workers close to starving, the unions finally acquiesced – the General Strike was over.

In agreeing to return to work, the strikers were vulnerable to reprisals from the employers, if not against individuals, then against the imposition of new working practices and wage structures enforced on them. In the settlement, the government were quick to explain that they could not guarantee that workers would be taken back on the same terms and conditions as before. Some employers used the fact that many of the strikers were on their last resources to enforce draconian wage cuts and conditions.

Aware of the potential damage that had been done to Britain because of the General Strike, Mussolini had passed legislation in Italy to ensure that a similar situation could not happen there.

> All strikes and lock-outs are forbidden, disputes being brought before special labour courts, whose decisions cannot be appealed against. The Press unanimously

> hails this action as the greatest work accomplished by the Fascist Cabinet. It is prophesised that other nations will soon follow Italy's lead by passing laws making it as unthinkable for capital and labour to settle their disputes by means of strikes or lock-outs, as it would be for two individuals to settle their private disputes by physical violence.

From the point of view of the two fascist groups, the BF and the British National Fascisti, the result was something of an anti-climax. Their entire existence had been based upon the fear that Britain was about to experience a revolution, a coup, and fall victim to socialism. They had promoted the British Empire as being the target of the Bolsheviks, who wanted to impose their view of how the world should be run on a free and autonomous people, and whose first step was to have been by way of a General Strike, unleashing the twin evils of communism and internationalism upon the modern cradle of democracy.

The fear of a revolution had been proved to be unfounded, and in the most public of ways. They had been convinced that their role during the struggle would involve physical resistance, similar to that seen in Italy during Mussolini's threatened march on Rome, perhaps even being offered a part in government as a result. The rule of law was something that the fascists had not reckoned on; the fact that a simple legal process had been sufficient to halt the strike without the need for bloodshed and that the police and army stood firmly behind the elected government negated the fear of revolution.

It was quite obvious that the difference between the fascist movements in Britain and Italy was the passion that could be generated by having a charismatic leader at its head. The British National Fascisti never really recovered following the General Strike, attempting to continue in the same manner as before the strike. Internal arguments within the leadership meant that it was wound up within two years and disappeared from the political consciousness. The BF did have a recognisable leader in Rotha Lintorn-Orman but not a charismatic one. The years that followed the ending of the General Strike were spent in reflection. Rotha still had her female troops, ready and keen to steward conservative meetings and to disrupt communist ones, but would otherwise concentrate on her other great passion, fighting against Irish independence.

In December of 1926, shortly after the coal miners ended their industrial action, a by-election in Smethwick saw Oswald Mosley returned to Westminster as a Labour MP. His tenure was to be one of dissention and upset, as ever falling out with the leadership, insistent that the Labour Party should bend to his views. A rapid rise through the ranks would massage his ego to the point where he would see himself as on a par with Mussolini and Hitler, but without the personality to take it to its ultimate conclusion.

The losing candidate in the by-election, a Mr Pike, blamed his defeat on systematic rowdyism denying him free speech.

> The public seemed hypnotised by my opponent's worldly possessions, and therefore did not see the irony of the Unionist candidate with plain record as a worker, fighting the Socialist who was everything the Labour Party condemns in theory at least. The main lesson of this election is that the conquest of the Labour Party by wealthy aristocrats has begun. While, therefore, I deplore the Smethwick result, I consider it far less serious for the government than for the Labour Party, which has gone clean away from its principles and lost the claim which was the basis of its strength – the claim to be a real working-class party.

CHAPTER 7

A PLETHORA OF PARTIES

When Arnold Leese separated from the British Fascists to join the British National Fascisti, he had found a group with which he felt comfortable. An only child, he was born in Lancashire in 1878, and trained as a veterinary surgeon, becoming a leading authority on the care of camels. During the war he served in the Royal Army Veterinary Corps in Somaliland and to France for the Advanced Horse Transport Depot. At the end of the war, he practised as a vet in Stamford, living there with his wife Winifred.

He joined the British Fascists as one of the early members, founding his own branch in Stamford shortly after. He then joined the Centre International d'Etudes sur le Fascisme, based in Switzerland, acting as their British correspondent for some time. One of his close neighbours was Arthur Kitson, the economist, who was declared bankrupt in 1925, for which he blamed Jewish bankers. Indeed he blamed Jewish bankers for most of the world's ills. Kitson gave Leese a copy of the book *The Protocols of the Elders of Zion*, since shown to be fake, which claimed to detail a Zionist plan to take over the world. Leese accepted it as truth without reservation.

Leese developed a Stamford branch quickly, and in 1924 responded to the local elections in the town by standing as a fascist, alongside another member of the branch, Harry Simpson.

> In the municipal elections at Stamford Lincs, two candidates were put forward by the local branch of

> the British Fascists to contest the apathy which would otherwise have enabled two Labour members to retain their seats unopposed. In both wards they were successful. The names of the new town councillors are Mr. A.S. Leese and Mr. H.L. Simpson. British Fascists from all over the country are to hold a great meeting in Trafalgar Square to-morrow.

Leese was not happy with the BF's policies, thinking them not extreme enough to reflect his own fascist and antisemitic views. He described them as being conservative with knobs on, not unlike Blakeney's analogy to the boy scouts. He was persuaded that the policies of the British National Fascisti were more suited to his beliefs and so he joined that group in preference; Simpson went with him. That group operated throughout the General Strike, but finally disintegrated and so Arnold Leese then formed the Fascist League from the remnants of the Stamford branch.

He and Simpson served only a single term as town councillors before resigning. Leese also retired from his veterinary practice and moved to Guildford in Surrey. During his retirement he had the opportunity to consider *The Britons* and its founder Henry Hamilton Beamish, a well-established anti-Jewish campaigner. In fact Beamish's organisation, while not claiming to be fascist, was perhaps the oldest antisemitic organisation of the modern period, attracting Arthur Kitson and Brigadier Blakeney among others. By the time that Leese retired, Beamish had moved to Southern Rhodesia and left John Henry Clarke in charge.

A word here about Arthur Kitson. Born in 1859, he was known as an authority on monetary theory, but still managed to be declared bankrupt in 1925. Kitson then became convinced that Jewish bankers had been the cause of his bankruptcy, and this heavily supported his already antisemitic views. In order to expound this view he sent a copy of *The Protocols of the Elders of Zion* to the American poet Ezra

Pound. Moving to Italy, Pound spoke against 'usury' and the Jewish plot of world domination, finding a ready audience there in the form of Benito Mussolini.

The aim of *The Britons*, the publication of British National Fascisti, was said to be the removal of all Jews from Britain and their resettlement in Palestine, although how that aim was to be achieved was seen by some as open to interpretation. Their main activity was by means of propaganda, publishing articles in various of their own journals such as *The British Guardian* and *Jewry Uber Alles*. Despite attempts to widen the appeal and promote anti-Jewish sentiment, *The Britons* never really rallied enough support to sustain it after the General Strike. Instead, it became little more than a publisher, and continued production of *The Protocols of the Elders of Zion* until its eventual demise.

> Over a period of many centuries a plot has been in operation to place all political power firmly in the hands of those who alone are qualified to use it properly – and that means in the hands of the Elders of Zion. Much has already been achieved but the plot hasn't yet reached fruition. Before the Elders can establish their rule over the whole world the existing Gentile states, which are already seriously undermined, must be finally abolished; and the Elders have a very precise idea as to how this is to be accomplished.
>
> In the first place everything possible must be done, in each existing state, to foster discontent and unrest. Fortunately the very nature of liberalism makes this easy. Already, by encouraging the incessant chatter with which parliaments fill their days, the Elders are helping to produce complete mental confusion in the populace. The very existence of a multiplicity of political parties helps. This increases the confusion in the popular mind and the

> Elders encourage this confusion by secretly supporting all these political parties. And then the Elders will also exert themselves to alienate the people from their rulers. In particular they will keep the workers in perpetual unrest by, on the one hand, sympathising with their grievances while, on the other hand, contriving to raise the cost of living, so that the grievances grow and grow.

The Protocols of the Elders of Zion was completely fabricated by an unknown person or group, suggesting that it contained details of an international Jewish plot to take over the world. In fact it was largely plagiarised from several earlier sources. The text was exposed as fraudulent by *The Times* in 1921, but continues to be credited by antisemitic groups as a genuine document, even having been described as the most influential work of antisemitism ever written. It appears to have emanated from Russia some time before the end of the nineteenth century and claims to be a record of a conference that discussed the future Jewish domination of the world.

Arnold Leese, now completely antisemitic in his views, as well as being against the socialists and communists, modelled his beliefs upon those of Mussolini in Italy. He formed a new organisation, the Imperial Fascist League, which reflected Leese's own feelings about Jews, to the point where one issue alone dominated the direction that the organisation took. This took him even further away from Rotha Lintorn-Orman, who defiantly refused to entertain antisemitic policies within the British Fascists, and the British National Fascisti, who professed the same leanings as Leese, but were no more in existence.

Arnold Leese believed that the different races could be separated into 'fighting' and 'non-fighting' according to their ability to engage in self-sacrifice and acquit themselves with honour. Thus, the Indians or Irish had no claim to nationality, and should be happy to simply live under Aryan rule. Similarly he believed that what he called the 'slave races' could never stand on equal terms with the British, since their 'undesirable' traits were fixed and transmitted by inheritance. Leese advocated austere and explicit domination of them on the basis of British racial supremacy.

Dennis Erskine-Tullock explained the Imperial Fascist League in a letter or press release, describing himself as the Commandant General with an address in London. The final few sentences of the letter implies that many members of the general public held fascist views, but were not registered as members of any established group.

> The Imperial Fascist League is the one organisation consecrated to the service of the British race and Empire in every sphere of national activity. The League is the result of the amalgamation of a number of Fascist organisations in this country, and is grouped into three branches: (1) the Lictors Association (open to nominated members only); (2) the Fascist Legions (the militant divided into active and reserve branches): (3) the Activists (the economic and industrial branch of the League) classified into three confederations of (a) employers. (b) employees. and (c) professional workers. On application from any of your readers who may be interested the undersigned will be pleased to send full particulars of the League, together with a copy of the *Tribune*, the organ of the movement. May we also urge all unattached Fascists in the district to communicate with us with a view to joining the local branch of the League.

Leese and the Imperial Fascist League became more and more obsessed about the danger from Jews undermining British institutions. Leese travelled to Germany where he met Julius Streicher, a leading follower of Adolf Hitler, and one who had an influential role within the journal *Der Stürmer*. Streicher was obsessed with the violation of German women by Jewish men, something he featured in *Der Stürmer*, which only served to increase its readership due to graphic recounting of such incidents. On his return, Leese modified the journal of the Imperial Fascist League along the lines of *Der Stürmer*.

Following Leese's visit to Germany, he became particularly obsessed with the concept of the Aryan race, something that he and Julius Streicher had in common. The concept of the Aryan race comes from the nineteenth-century wish to identify the original northern European population, as against those who could not claim that ancestry. Among those who fell outside that term Aryan were the Jews, and the term was used by the fascists to point to the constant struggle that existed between Aryans and Jews, later to be incorporated within the Nazi creed.

> In Europe the notion of white racial superiority emerged in the 1850s, propagated most assiduously by the Comte de Gobineau and later by his disciple Houston Stewart Chamberlain, who first used the term "Aryan" to mean the "white race". Members of that so-called race spoke Indo-European languages, were credited with all the progress that benefited humanity, and were purported to be superior to "Semites", "yellows", and "blacks". Believers in Aryanism came to regard the Nordic and Germanic peoples as the purest members of the "race". That notion, which had been repudiated by anthropologists by the second quarter of the 20th century, was seized upon by Adolf Hitler and the Nazis and was made the basis of the German Government policy of exterminating Jews, Roma (Gypsies), and other "non-Aryans".

Leese's extreme views extended to offering views on how to solve the Jewish question, something he could not persuade Oswald Mosley to accept. Leese was of the opinion that Mosley was not as convinced as he that the Jews were so manipulative as to attempt to take over the worldwide banking system and hold the Aryan races to ransom. Leese's solution was to exterminate the Jews, by rounding them up and dispatching them by way of gas chambers, a chilling reminder of what happened in Germany and central Europe during the Nazi era. When Mosley did not agree, Leese and the Imperial Fascist League decided to remain as a separate entity.

The publication of *The Fascist*, the journal of the Imperial Fascist League, continued to be the literary outlet for Arnold Leese's antisemitic views. Among them were that Jews were responsible for the murder of Christian children during the Passover as well as his proposal for the use of gas chambers in solving the Jewish problem. This outburst resulted in him being given a six-month prison sentence for seditious libel; his accomplice, Walter Whitehead, was fined. The judge at the trial had a few choice words for Leese.

> I am satisfied that nothing can be more mischievous to the public weal than the circulation of statements of this kind. I can appreciate that behind what you have done there is possibly a belief amounting in its intensity almost to fanaticism with regard to the truth or otherwise of these statements. That the public well-being can be served by the publication of stuff of this kind – and I call it "stuff" advisably – I cannot imagine. Nothing can be more harmful to the public weal than that.

Following that experience, Leese maintained his antisemitic views within the confines of the Imperial Fascist League, not allowing other groups to influence their further development. Leese still expounded them, but they remained the product of his particular beliefs, and unmodified by others. Both he and Rotha Lintorn-Orman separated their groups from others expounding similar views. Neither of the two would work with the rising star of the fascist movement,

Oswald Mosley, nor would they work with one another. While all three included dislike of the Jews within their remit, there existed an impassible void as to the extent.

After the General Strike, and the disappointment of not being called upon to defend the country against revolution, Rotha Lintorn-Orman turned her attention to that other bone of contention, Northern Ireland. The Irish Free State had been created in 1922, before the British Fascists had come into being, as a dominion of the British Empire. It was made up of twenty-six of the thirty-two counties, the other six counties remaining as part of Britain, and was the outcome of the three-year-long Irish War of Independence.

Even with the creation of the Irish Free State the conflict continued, the sticking point being that members of the Dáil, the Irish parliament, were required to take an oath of allegiance to the constitution of the Irish Free State and to declare fidelity to the King. The government finally overcame the anti-treaty faction and the Sinn Féin president Éamon de Valera resigned from that party and formed the new Fianna Fáil, and entered the Dáil. Under the treaty a governor-general was appointed to advise the king and the oath of allegiance was to be to the king in Ireland, not in England. This took some of the sting out of the situation.

While not being of significance to the fascist movement, the preservation of the British Empire was of fundamental importance to Rotha Lintorn-Orman and the conservative group that had formed around her. The British Fascists had resisted attempts to be diverted from its original task, that of preserving the status quo, confirming its ultra-conservative origins. It was not antisemitic, although individual members may have had extremist notions. It was pro-government, providing the government was not tainted with beliefs of socialism and internationalism. It advocated using force where the government was too weak to resist the Bolsheviks, or too blind to recognise the danger.

Now, with the Irish Free State seeking to separate itself from the British Empire, Rotha was convinced that it was her duty to resist such a move. She found support amongst conservatives in Ireland who saw the severing of all ties with Britain as disloyalty to the king and, as such, disloyalty to the country. She began campaigning in Northern Ireland, currying support from all those who had been against the establishment of the Irish Free State, and even more so against the idea of full Irish independence.

During her visits to Northern Ireland she spoke out against the rise in socialism and warned of the apathy allowing Bolshevism to take hold. She argued against 'internationalism' and urged financial support for British manufactured items and agricultural produce and the idea of removing foreigners from the country in order to provide jobs for British workers, and investment by and for British industry. In other words, the same message that she was giving to the mainland, except that she was a visitor in Ireland and was a little more circumspect in the tone of her delivery.

> The Fascists maintained that this country was getting nearly as bad as Italy used to be before Mussolini came into power, and it was up to them to he prepared – to fight the Reds or else they would find themselves involved in a war very much worse than the ghastly affair of 1914. One type of person, said Miss Orman, that the Fascists had no use for was the conscientious objector. This "no more war" talk that a large number were spreading about could only be described as sloppy sentiment. Britain was the bulwark standing before the Red horror, and when the British Empire was destroyed, then civilisation was doomed. In conclusion, Miss Orman repeated that the Fascists were a non-political non-party organisation. They took an oath of loyalty to their King which they were prepared to keep to the bitter end. They urged people to buy British goods and were determined that aliens should be removed from this

> country so that British subjects could have the jobs they were entitled to.

In Somerset she made her home at Over Langford Manor the centre for her all-women shock troops. It was in Somerset that they trained on weekend camps in Rotha's estate. Back in London they occupied, or amused, themselves breaking up meetings of rival groups, such as those of the socialists or the communists, and even of other fascist groups such as the Imperial Fascist League. It was while breaking up one such meeting that they met opposition, not only from Arnold Leese's group but also from Oswald Mosley's Blackshirts, who were on a similar mission. The result was a three-way fight at which some blood was spilt.

There were some attempts made to rejuvenate the British Fascists, but the membership was beginning to drift away to the more extreme groups, with Leese or Mosley at their head. Rotha Lintorn-Orman had never been the charismatic leader that the British Fascists had needed. Instead it was seen to be led, as one would expect, by a committee. There were attempts to introduce an element of antisemitism, but with an ethos of ultra-conservatism as their prime motivation, it was resisted by the rank and file.

The end of the British Fascists came with the failing in health of Rotha Lintorn-Orman, who had become dependent on alcohol and drugs, to the point that her mother began to reduce the money she was prepared to spend on financing her daughter's political movement. By this time it must have become obvious that Rotha's group was never going to become the country's leading fascist organisation. Many of its rivals embraced issues which fell outside of her own ideas. Many of the original ultra-conservatives remained loyal to her, including Viscountess Downe, but the writing was clearly on the wall for the British Fascists.

Rotha set sail for Las Palmas in early 1935 and a few weeks later died in the village of Santa Brígida, not far from Las Palmas (visiting had become her routine in recent winters). She was buried there in the English Cemetery, alone and disillusioned, leaving the fascist cause to be fought over by Leese and Mosley, but over the ideals, not of Mussolini but of Hitler. There was little in the British press to mark her passing, but there was a reference in Ireland.

> Miss R.L. Lintorn-Orman, a great friend of Ulster, passed away at Las Palmas on March 10, 1935. Daughter of the late Major Charles Orman and granddaughter of the late Field-Marshal Sir Lintorn Simmons, she worked during the war for the women's reserve ambulance, the Scottish Women's Hospital Corps, with which she sailed for active service in Siberia in 1916. She served on the Drina Front as an ambulance driver, and was awarded the Croix de Charitie (twice) for gallantry. In 1917, on being invalided home, she joined the British Red Cross Society, and was appointed commandant in charge of the motor school at Devonshire House, where she won golden opinions for her efficiency. To fight Communism, she founded in May 1923, the organisation known as British Fascists, and during the General Strike in 1926 members could not be enrolled quickly enough. Miss Lintorn-Orman was an ardent Loyalist, and, connected with the Loyal Orange Order in Ulster, spoke at the July celebrations in 1930.

An interesting event recorded in some of the provincial newspapers was a visit by the Prince of Wales, later to become Edward VIII, to the White City to attend the British Industries Fair. He was accompanied by his mother, the queen, and his brother Prince George. When they arrived, they were met by a number of Fascists who gave the fascist salute – the right arm outstretched – which Edward returned in the same manner. This may have been a very early indication of where Edward's real sympathies lay.

In Britain great changes were taking place within industry and commerce. Recession in Britain had been a continuation of what was happening all over the world, with the difference being that this 'bust' had not been preceded by a 'boom'. There were few fortunes to be lost, because few fortunes had been made. Britain had never fully recovered from the General Strike of 1926, never really made up lost ground from the First World War, and had come to realise that America's policy of isolation was not going to come to its aid.

Other industrial countries in Europe had found a political answer to their troubles by adopting a new form of government, a form of government which demanded too high a price for the reward it offered. In Italy it had been delivered by Mussolini, in Germany by Hitler, in Spain it would be Franco. But even as the First World War was ending Russia, under Lenin, had seen its solution in another form of totalitarian government – communism. Again the freedom of the individual being sacrificed for the benefit of the state.

The supposed beneficiaries of totalitarian government were those who fell below the median line. In Russia, with its vast rural peasant population, it was fairly easy to identify them, and in Italy and Germany it was the unskilled factory workers. In Russia the aristocracy were the villains, in Italy, the bloated capitalists and in Germany the Jewish financiers. In Britain it was not likely that the Russian model would be followed, despite the fears of the ultra-conservatives. More likely the threat would come from the Italian, or possibly, the German model. Britain's best defence lay within her middle class and her skilled and semi-skilled factory workforce.

This was the time when Britain, at last, awoke to the impending threat of fascism, and saw the formation of specific anti-fascist groups, mainly as a response to Oswald Mosley's growing popularity. These were, in the main, offshoots from the Communist Party, which felt particularly targeted. In Germany, Hitler was in the process of violating the Treaty of Versailles by establishing the Luftwaffe and generally re-arming. He also introduced the Nuremberg Laws

Above left: Sir Arthur Conan Doyle.

Above right: Rudyard Kipling.

Right: Emmeline Pankhurst.

Charles Cooper Penrose-Fitzgerald.

Field Marshal Lord Kitchener.

Above: Factory work.

Right: Rotha Lintorn-Orman.

Alan Ian Percy, Duke of Northumberland.

Benito Mussolini.

Above left: Oswald Mosley.

Above right: Arnold Leese.

Right: Ramsay MacDonald.

Above left: William Morris, Lord Nuffield.

Above right: Diana Mosley.

Left: Unity Mitford.

Above left: William Joyce,
Lord Haw-Haw.

Above right: General Franco.

Right: King Edward VIII.

Above left: Winston Churchill.

Above right: David Freeman-Mitford, Baron Redesdale.

The emblem of the British Union of Fascists.

by which Jews were denied many of their rights, specifically of citizenship and of marriage between Jews and non-Jews. In Italy, Mussolini invaded Abyssinia (Ethiopia), much to the annoyance of the League of Nations, and in Spain tension was growing between the socialists and the army, led by Francisco Franco.

The League of Nations had been founded in 1920, based on an idea by President Woodrow Wilson. Although it was intended to prevent future wars, it never managed to have more than sixty member countries at any one time, and therefore was never in a position to enforce its decisions. A major flaw was that individual alliances took priority over the League's decisions. This was compounded by the fact that, although it was the American head of state that was its guiding light, America declined ever to become a member.

The stage was set for a political standoff within Britain; on the one side the rule of law, and a duly elected government that was trying to negotiate a way to navigate a Europe that had expansion as its prime motive; on the other side a fascist who would join Hitler's antisemitic desire to solve the Jewish problem at a stroke. Ahead lay a period of conflict and domestic upheaval, and a period of appeasement to hold Hitler at bay. Internment would become a matter of fact, and conscription would be reintroduced. There would be no need for a second White Feather Brigade and no call for volunteers to join the army. Again, women would play their part in saving Britain.

CHAPTER 8

THE NEW PARTY

Oswald Mosley had been married to Lady Cynthia Curzon since 1922 – both were titled, and were unlikely supporters of the Independent Labour Party. Indeed, during the campaign, the right-wing newspapers had attacked him for preaching socialism whilst wearing a suit from Savile Row, and his wife for attending functions in a dress that glittered with diamonds. Described as champagne socialists, they were criticised for living a debauched lifestyle on the French Riviera, and Oswald Mosley for never having done a day's work in his life.

Cynthia corresponded with Leon Trotsky, who she admired. The two met in Prinkipo, Turkey, but Trotsky was suspicious of her husband, who was forever sniping at Ramsay MacDonald's leadership, referring to Mosley as an 'aristocratic coxcomb'. The Labour government had refused Trotsky political asylum in Britain and Cynthia had used this in order to make common ground between them, plus flattering him a little on his recent autobiography.

Both the Mosleys had been members of the Labour Party since 1924 and had fought the 1929 General Election, he winning Smethwick and she Stoke-on-Trent, both becoming Labour MPs. They had been long-term members of the Fabian Society, seeking to promote the ideas of socialism and fairness in society without the threat of revolution. As someone who had previously been an MP, albeit a Conservative MP, Oswald Mosley had expected to be given one of the Great Offices of State by Ramsay MacDonald, but was made only Chancellor of the Duchy of Lancaster without portfolio. Having been given responsibility for solving Britain's unemployment problem, a mighty task, he found that what initiatives he proposed met obstructions from the Cabinet as a whole, or at least from the Lord Privy Seal.

This was contrary to the initial reception he had from Labour in 1924. Then, he had been lauded both for finding Labour views more to his liking than those of the Conservatives, and also that he rejected the beliefs of his own class. The Labour prime minister, Ramsay MacDonald, feeling that Mosley could help substantiate the belief that Labour was worthy of the country's trust, and also add a little magic to its image, might have been expected to be more supportive of Mosley and his ideas.

Ramsay MacDonald was not as impressed with his ideas as Mosley would have expected, which led to him, in 1930, publishing his thoughts in the Mosley Memorandum. Mosley's ideas were not much different from the fascist ones promoted by Mussolini in Italy, including his growing fear of globalization or internationalism, and the growing dependence upon international finance and financiers. Despite being rejected by the Labour Party, the memorandum was praised by many of the leading economists of the time, including John Maynard Keynes, who wrote:

> I like the spirit which informs the document. A scheme of national economic planning to achieve a right, or at least a better, balance of our industries between the old and the new, between agriculture and manufacture, between home development and foreign investment; and wide executive powers to carry out the details of such a scheme. That is what it amounts to... the manifesto offers us a starting point for thought and action. . . It will shock – it must do so – the many good citizens of this country … who have laissez-faire in their craniums, their consciences,

> and their bones ... but how anyone professing and calling himself a socialist can keep away from the manifesto is a more obscure matter.

Later in the year, Mosley had an opportunity to lay his thoughts before the Labour Party at the annual conference. Again the Mosley Memorandum was rejected. With unemployment standing at two and a half million the Labour government was beginning to fall apart; reliance on MPs to find a solution was beginning to prove misplaced. Mussolini's belief in having experts, rather than politicians, to make the really big decisions was appearing to offer some sense. The British parliamentary system had long been criticised by the extreme left in politics, as well as by the extreme right, and it seemed that the idea of fracturing some of the old doctrines of the political system might not be totally without merit.

> The group of members of Parliament, headed by Sir Oswald Mosley, whose intention to resign from the Labour party was reported yesterday, met last night and decided to continue the existence of the group, individual members being free to take whatever action they thought fit. Sir Oswald Mosley will issue a statement at the end of the week as to his personal intentions, but it is now stated that only four of the seventeen members of the group will resign, including Sir Oswald Mosley and his wife, Lady Cynthia Mosley.

Mosley resigned from the Labour Party, forming a new political party which, appropriately, he named the New Party. He was joined by six others, all Labour MPs, including his wife Cynthia, Robert Forgan and John Strachey. Two others, Oliver Baldwin and W.J. Brown, left the New Party within a day to sit as independents. Lord Nuffield, otherwise William Morris of Morris Motors Ltd., financed the New

Party to the strength of £50,000. Morris also financed a magazine, *Action,* to support the New Party, under Harold Nicolson, an ex-diplomat and open homosexual.

William Morris was well known as being anti-union and antisemitic, although his motor car factories in Oxford suffered from industrial action on numerous occasions. In Britain he was regarded as the most famous industrialist of his age. He had been born in a working-class district of Worcester and began his working life apprenticed to a bicycle repair company, setting up on his own, aged sixteen, in his father's shed and then bought his first shop. He expanded into motorcycles and then motorcars in 1912.

The manifesto of the New Party quite clearly contained much of Mussolini's model of fascism, including the need for a disciplined corps of fit young men to counter the threat of communism. The main thrust was an economical one, the imposition of high tariffs to protect British industry and agriculture, and the nationalisation of strategic industries such as coal mining and steel production. To counter the scourge of unemployment, the New Party recommended that the school leaving age should be raised so that the work force was reduced.

One of the tenets of Mussolini's model of fascism, and one that Mosley adopted enthusiastically, was that political control should be in the hands of a small inner cabinet, under a charismatic leader, the members of which were not individually subject to elections, rather appointed as experts in their field. The leader was to be appointed for life, and the small cabinet drawn from outside Parliament – in effect the leader, for example Mosley, being appointed for life with no mechanism for replacement.

> Sir Oswald Mosley ... announced the formation of the New Party. He seeks to mobilise at least 400 candidates to fight at the next election. The statement declared that sufficient support in Parliament and in the country

> is already assured to justify the launching of the organisation ... we challenge the fifty-year-old system of Free Trade which exposes industry in the home market to the chaos of world conditions, such as price fluctuation, dumping, and the competition of sweated labour, which result in the lowering of wages and industrial decay ... we challenge also the century old system of protection which Conservatives seek to put in the place of Free Trade, with the result that the employer alone will be protected and entrenched at the expense of both worker and consumer.

Events quickly overtook the Labour government with the depression causing the financial collapse of the European banks and the subsequent withdrawal of capital from London. To avoid a devaluation of sterling, Ramsay MacDonald, needing to secure foreign loans, was forced to promise a balanced budget, reducing nearly all the promised spending reforms. Finally the Labour Party rejected MacDonald's plan, which left him no alternative but to offer his resignation. With no enthusiasm to take on this unpopular task, it was finally decided that a coalition of Labour, Conservative and Liberal MPs, under Ramsay MacDonald, would take office under the title of the National Government.

A letter from Ernest Winterton to Ramsay MacDonald expressed the sentiments of many Labour MPs, mentioning also the political issues involving India's struggle for independence from British rule, particularly the civil disobedience movement.

> I wish to thank you for your letter ... in which you ask me to suspend judgement on the situation which has arisen and the steps you have taken to meet it. I am certainly prepared to do that as regards the unrevealed "sacrifices" which, I understand, the new government is to call for. I do not believe, however, that a low standard of living can

> never assist prosperity. If national financial stability is to be attained, no more delusive method of attempting to secure it can be suggested than to "economise" on those who already have so little purchasing power that their poverty is a menace to all who must live by production. You will see therefore that I cannot contemplate "economies" of this character, and on this issue I must perforce oppose the proposals of your newly formed government with all the influence I can exert. This does not prevent me from recognising the sincerity of your own position, and my only regret is that I fear the step you have taken may gravely jeopardise the chances of crowning your life's work for peace in the coming disarmament year and of securing that wise settlement of the Indian Problem to which you have devoted so much patient and unremitting labour during the past months.

The next General Election was set for October 1931, which gave Oswald Mosley an opportunity to prepare his potential candidates for the contest. Just prior to the election, Mosley was unwell and had taken himself off to the Riviera to recover but then returned immediately the election was called. There were twenty-five candidates for the New Party, Mosley standing in his wife's old constituency of Stoke-on-Trent, she not seeking re-election. The left-wing vote was split between the New Party and Labour, both appealing to the working-class voter, both in favour of protectionism in the form of high import duties on foreign goods and by restricting the number of foreign workers competing for fewer and fewer jobs. The election was easily won by the coalition and a new National Government, under Ramsay MacDonald, was formed.

The National Government set themselves three initial targets; to devalue sterling, to keep interest rates low and to impose tariffs in an attempt to reduce inflation. The imposition of tariffs caused a corresponding tit-for-tat loss of exports. Trade with the Empire was already decreasing, and the protectionist policies caused a further decline. Agricultural subsidies were increased, but this did not bring about the growth anticipated. Strangely, the fascist policy of protectionism, which had been one of the cornerstones of Mosley's campaign, was the first to fail.

The New Party did not win a single seat in 1931, and Mosley was forced to accept that his party had suffered complete defeat at the polls. However he could rationalise that it was not the wrong message, but the wrong timing that had prevented him from being able to fully capitalise on Labour's failings. It was a cabal made up of Stanley Baldwin, Ramsey MacDonald, Lloyd George and the king that had managed to bring about the National Government. It was this unfortunate timing that had prevented the New Party from capitalising on the failings of Ramsey MacDonald's mistakes while leader of the Labour Party.

In order to develop new strategies to promote his ideas, Mosley visited Italy early the following year. He met with Mussolini, saw many of the achievements made, and was much impressed by them, and by him. Mosley returned to Britain, more convinced than ever that the Italian model of fascism was the one most suited to Britain. He wound up the New Party and embarked on fascism as the most likely option to bring Britain out of recession. He was still receiving overtures from the main parties to join them and work from within to achieve results, but he resisted them in the belief that they were too reactionary to change. Mosley wanted change to come quickly, and this could be best achieved with his efforts alone.

During the summer of 1932 Mosley wrote down his vision of the future shape of British politics, his vision of Britain's fascist future, and how to bring Britain out of the depression that it was experiencing. He was particularly concerned about the high levels of unemployment which at the time of writing was over one million and had been as high as two million. He claimed that the economic growth of the country had outgrown the political institutions that controlled it, indicating that the government, in its present form, was incapable of governing efficiently. His view was that Britain had never fully recovered from the war, in part owing to an outdated form of government.

> But there is no room for interests which are not the State's interests; laws are futile if they allow such things to be. Wise laws, and wise institutions, are those which harness without restricting; which allow human activity full play but guide it into channels which serve the nation's ends. Hence the need for a New Movement, not only in politics, but in the whole of our national life. The movement is Fascist, (i) because it is based on a high conception of citizenship ideals as lofty as those which inspired the reformers of a hundred years ago: (ii) because it recognises the necessity for an authoritative state, above party and sectional interests.

He made some comments about Rotha Lintorn-Orman and British Fascists, claiming that she had misused the name, while not fully understanding the concept, regarding it as meaning ultra-conservative and reactionary, rather than constructive and revolutionary. He said that it should combine the dynamic urge for change and progress with authority, discipline and order, without which nothing great could be achieved. The essence of fascism is the power of adaptation to fresh facts, it is a realistic creed, it is a steel creed of an 'iron age'.

> Fascism is Dictatorship in the modern sense of the word, which implies government armed by the people with power to solve problems which the people are determined to overcome. Modern Dictatorship implements the will of the people to action which cannot be implemented without

> the power of action being entrusted to government. In this sense we accept the word Dictatorship but we do not accept it in the sense implied by our opponents. By Dictatorship we mean Leadership; by Dictatorship they mean tyranny.

Mosley was of the opinion that in countries such as Italy and Germany things had been allowed to drift so far towards collapse and anarchy that, when the fascists had come to power, more rigorous measures were needed than would be necessary in Britain. The rigour of a fascist government would be in very exact proportion to the degree of chaos which preceded it. He said that Britain was great enough to adopt fascism because it would choose fascism, before it had to adopt it by reason of national collapse.

> Most of the Bills before Parliament demand technical knowledge; but they are discussed, voted on, and their fate decided, by men and women chosen for their assiduity in opening local charity bazaars, or for their lung power at street corners. This is by no means an over-statement; when a young man asks his Party Executive for a constituency, they do not ask "will he be a good member?", but "will he be a good candidate?" Government must have power to legislate by order to carry out the will of the majority without the organised obstruction of minorities who at present use Parliamentary procedure to frustrate the will of the nation. We must eliminate the solemn humbug of six hundred men and women indulging in detailed debate of every technical measure, handled by a non-technical assembly in a vastly technical age.

On the subject of liberty, Mosley suggested that the only liberty the ordinary man desired was the freedom to live in a decent house, earn good wages for reasonable hours of work such as not to leave him exhausted, unmolested private happiness with his wife, children and friends and, finally, the hope of material success to set the seal on private ambition. But many were unemployed, with the remainder living in the shadow of unemployment, low wages, long hours, bad housing and diminishing social amenities.

On the subject of parliamentary government, Mosley was dismissive of debate, in that the speakers held no illusions of persuasion, but were merely trying to grandstand themselves to their electors, and to please their party whips. These, after all, financed the candidates and were quick to reject them should they not tow the party line. In complicated affairs, somebody must be trusted, or nothing would ever be done. To some, it might signal the suppression of liberty, to others, the suppression of chaos.

> We have seen the political parties of the old democracy collapse into futility through the sterility of committee government and the cowardice and irresponsibility of their leadership. Voluntary discipline is the essence of the modern movement. Leadership in fascism may be an individual or a team, but undoubtedly single leadership in practice proves the more effective instrument ... the only effective instrument of revolutionary change is absolute authority.

The nature of government, according to Mosley, would be radically changed. Having first won a legal election, MPs (fascist) would be appointed as local executive officers in the area they represent. Too many times the local government obstructed the national government's will and this measure would effectively put an end to this conflict. Similarly the House of Lords would be changed to be appointed by fascist nominees, technically qualified, later to be elected on a purely technical basis, ensuring that political parties would have little or no influence.

> Opposition no longer serves the purposes of reasoned criticism and analysis of the government's policy which exposes weaknesses and elicits the verities of national problems. Modern problems are too technical by their very nature to be handled effectively by such an assembly. Debate, therefore, is no longer constructive but purely destructive and concentrated on transient issues of popular passions which tend yet further to obscure the real issues which should receive the attention of government.

Towards the end of his writings, Mosley affirmed his belief that a fascist Britain would have no room for the drone and the decadent, who used their leisure to destroy their capacity for public usefulness. If an action did not harm the country or its citizens, and if it left one sound in mind and body, it could not then be morally wrong. Happiness must also be an ambition: enjoying a drink in the pub, watching a football match, going to the cinema or going to a racecourse. Providing they are not enjoyed to excess, these indulgencies were to be encouraged. As long as they did not squander their health or resources, it contributed to efficiency and service.

On the matter of the British Empire, Mosley was quite definite in his thoughts. He was of the opinion that the established political parties were each guilty of betrayal and surrender. Previous invaders of India had brought, not the constructive and beneficial achievements of British rule, but atrocities against the original inhabitants of India, who they virtually obliterated.

> We have a right to stay in India and we intend to stay there. We have more than a right; we have a duty to stay there. We have a right because modern India owes everything to British rule. Irrigation, railways, schools, universities, hospitals, impartial justice, every amenity which makes modern life possible for any section of

> the inhabitants of India was conferred by the energy of the British Government.... Any withdrawal of British authority can only result in wide-spread destruction of life accompanied by unthinkable atrocities and ending in a relapse into barbarism. In such conditions the duty of Britain is as clear as her right; that duty is to remain and to govern.

Mosley blamed the established parties for the indecisions that had beset the country, something they had taken with them into the National Government; he said that they had no programme when they started, and they had no programme now. Their leaders had not foreseen the crisis of 1931 until it overwhelmed them, and indeed they derided the possibility of it happening.

Contained in his writings was a great amount of detailed information and extrapolation of figures to demonstrate how a fascist regime would bring wealth and prosperity to Britain. Mixed with that was much propaganda extolling the benefits of fascism and much criticism of the established political parties. He did not propose a new political party, but presented a manifesto for a union of the existing fascist parties – the British Union of Fascists (BUF). He said that antisemitism would not be an issue for the BUF and that they would not attack Jews simply on account of them being Jews.

Mosley claimed they would attack Jews if they were engaged in subversive activities, such as the direction of the Communist Party, or if they were engaged in international financial transactions such as those which had recently shaken Britain. Jews who were loyal citizens of Britain and who served the country, rather than its enemies, would always have a square deal from the BUF. On the subject of storm troopers, he said that they did have a band of strong young men, highly disciplined in a semi-militaristic manner, and available to defend BUF meetings. Such groups were unarmed, and never employed aggressively.

> A London antisemitic weekly, referred last Thursday to the meeting addressed by Sir Oswald Mosley, at which he made certain references to Jews: Sir Oswald Mosley made an excellent speech, which was in no way provocative, it says. Yet from the start there was organised Jewish interruption. In its way this meeting was an illustration of Jewish terrorism. Had there not been a very strong body of Blackshirts, the meeting would have been broken up before one word was said. The bullying of Jews was disgraceful. The disturbance was not Communist. In a corner of the gallery, close above the platform, was a gang of Jews who annoyed Sir Oswald Mosley all through his speech, and later had to be turned out. The quarrel was forced on the Fascists by the Jews, for Sir Oswald Mosley carefully avoided reference to the Jewish question. One Jew, on rising for the purpose of alleged heckling, saw fit to announce that he was a boxing man and a Rugby football player. Jewish terrorism in London has become a national danger, the paper concludes.... Immediately the place was in an uproar. I cannot make out why antisemitism should not be part of Sir Oswald's creed, the writer says, and I am sure he will get the worst of it every time if he and his adherents forget the traditional British notion of fair play.

After another meeting Mosley was greeted with cheers from his own supporters and boos and jeers from others. He then marched at the head of a procession up Fleet Street and along the Strand towards Westminster. A number of people who were following the marchers sang the 'Red Flag', to be countered by a rendition of 'Rule Britannia'. When the marchers reached Norfolk Street there was a brief tussle between the police and members of the rival factions. One man's face was cut and bruised, but no serious damage was done.

CHAPTER 9

CHARISMA

The British Fascisti was born out of a fear of socialist domination rather than a desire for change. When the ultra-conservatives gathered together in their drawing rooms to bemoan their situation, they wanted a return to the days before the war. Days when there was a respect for status, and of course money, but for an understanding and regard for the correct order of things. God had ordained who should govern, and who should obey; those who already had, should conserve their wealth, and those who had not, should continue in their subordinate role.

As the calendar turned from the immediate post-war years to the 1920s, the fear of socialism reared its head to threaten London drawing room sensitivities. In order to address their fears, they looked toward Italy, where a solution was being presented by Benito Mussolini, albeit controversial. His approach was very different to that which they envisaged under British moderation. Mussolini instigated three basic tenets: that the rights of the individual should be subjugated to those of the state; that government decisions should be taken by experts rather elected politicians; that there should be a charismatic unelected leader in order to drive the changes through.

Mussolini adopted the name fascist for his system. Rotha Lintorn-Orman adopted the same name for her British organisation, not because she intended to ape Mussolini, but because fascist was a word in current circulation. The two were not the same, but they were judged against the same yardstick: that of a totalitarian political force which would come to represent all that was bad in the world. Rotha Lintorn-Orman did not intend to overthrow the existing British government; her mission was to preserve it and prevent its further decay. Her supporters might be described as ultra-conservative, although some of them harboured a more extreme agenda.

Using the definition of fascism that described the Italian model, the BF presented a weak and ineffective version, leading those of a more extreme view to label it as boy scout fascism – unfair as it was yet to be defined. The word fascist in the title was destined to be interpreted by some as echoing the totalitarian dictatorship in Italy, with its Blackshirts and its tough squads of enforcers, calling them stewards.

The group largely adopted the trappings of Mussolini's popular cause, but not its ethos. Whereas Mussolini was in the process of taking over the government of Italy, Rotha had no such plans. She proclaimed a loyalty to the king and, providing its resolve did not weaken, to the government of the day. She saw the BF's role to be one of coming to the government's aid in time of need, defined as its continued resistance to socialist domination.

The BF, largely financed by Rotha's mother, was quick to relegate Rotha to the sidelines, leaving men to take over the reins; a trait which her young women members were accustomed to, and one which brought back memories of the fight for women's suffrage. In 1923 when the BF was formed, even in 1926 when the General Strike took place, women were still waiting for the 'vote', were still regarded as second class members of society, and deserving no place in politics. The young women who had stood as suffragettes, worked on the front line in Serbia or distributed white feathers were now pushed even further from having a hand in the decision process.

As time passed the more extreme members, male, left to form or join other organisations, some to become notorious in their new groups, others to be reduced to obscurity. While members were gradually lost, Rotha stealthily regained control, and gradually recovered the ultra-conservative ethos. As she did so she rallied groups of like-minded young women around her, alike in stature, in dress and in disregard for the male of the species.

Many women, disillusioned with male dominance in politics, rallied to a female figure at the helm. With male membership of BF melting away, fewer challenges to their leadership confronted Rotha and the other women. It could be argued that BF became increasingly a woman's organisation, exhibiting peevishness to its direct opposition, while being more tolerant toward those who simply did not support it.

The General Strike saw BF regain its original construct, refusing to adopt antisemitism, while still refusing to abandon its use of the term fascism. Other groups, gathering under the heading of fascist, emulated the Italian model more closely, with an eye cast towards Germany and the growing dominance of Hitler. Their function appeared to be one of strike-breaking, not directly against those who drove busses, delivered letters or manned vital offices, but against those who picketed their places of work. There was little evidence of strike-breakers making a real difference except in their public show of defiance.

Arnold Leese and the IFL played the major part in combatting the General Strike. It was they who gained the publicity with their blatant headlining stunts. It was they who protected the lorry depots, the newspaper vans, the food trucks etc. It was they who policed the larger Conservative Party meetings, who got into running fights with pickets, who attacked the strikers' rallies.

The BF were severely disappointed by the outcome of the General Strike, not because of its result, but because it proved that the socialist and communist threat was not as real as they had anticipated. Arnold Leese, who had led the fascist resistance, was reduced to provincial obscurity. Rotha turned her attention to Ireland, which left the field wide open for a new entrant, in fact a man with charisma who had been on the scene for some time, Oswald Mosley. Rotha Lintorn-

Orman refused Mosley's overtures to join him, so remained to plough her own lonely furrow.

The death of Rotha Lintorn-Orman meant the dissolution of the BF, and the end of her concept of fascism being an ultra-conservative movement. Instead, it established fascism in the Italian mould of a bullying regime, intent on its charismatic leader becoming all-powerful. Meanwhile another fascist regime was developing in Germany with its own ruthless leader at its head – Adolf Hitler. It was the German model which would present the threat to Britain in the years to come.

T.S. Elliot wrote:

> I did not feel very hopeful about the Mosley group myself. But the point is this: Mosley may have struck a bit too soon; but as things are drifting at present, it seems to me only a question of time before there is a popular movement towards some form of Hitlerism in England, and I want to think about it before it happens. For any strong definite cry may be the "programme"; it depends merely on circumstances whether the appeal is to revolution or to reaction, to Toryism or to Socialism. The actual Mosley programme seems to me to fall between two stools; it still aims at those who continue to believe that the whole difficulty can be settled by finding an economic dodge better than the dodges of Baldwin, George, Macdonald & Snowden, or than that of Keynes and the pundits, and who are willing to try any purely economic heresy so long as all their other beliefs are undisturbed. Now my instinct is that any heresy violent enough to save matters (and I believe matters to be in a much worse way than most people think) – cannot be a mere economic heresy – we are hardened to those – but must be something requiring real self sacrifice of the

> individual, whoever he be, to the common good; but I will not admit that the Common Good can any longer imply getting the better of some other nation's Common Good.

With the demise of BF, Britain lost the chance of regaining a degree of patriotism that could operate within acceptable boundaries. The concept of ultra-conservatism vanished, to be replaced by a dichotomy, on the one hand fascism in the Italian or German style; on the other hand, socialism or communism in the Russian style. Neither of these two options offered the London drawing room set with an acceptable model. It would take an event of great enormity to force Britain down a middle path.

CHAPTER 10

CONCENTRATING POWER

Oswald Mosley, in his manifesto, had confirmed his position as being completely committed to the fascist cause. His visits to Italy in 1932 and 1933 were an affirmation of his beliefs, taking much of the operational methods from Mussolini's structure of his supporters. Foremost amongst these was realising the need for a uniformed squad of men to secure his meetings from communists and others opposed to him. Taking a lead from Mussolini's Blackshirts, Mosley created a similar group in Britain. In reality they were a group of tough thugs who behaved similarly to the 'Black and Tans', whose conduct had first caused him to leave the Conservative Party in 1920.

Recruitment into the BUF Blackshirts was achieved by the very local nature of the organisation. Although the BUF was a nationwide organisation, it was run and operated on a district level. In the countryside this meant village by village, or parish by parish. Individual members knew one another, perhaps had been to the same school, worked on the same farm etc. In the cities, although the same applied, there were also groups based around sports clubs or special interest groups. This meant that individual members were not isolated and therefore not subject to reprisals within the locality. The district units were organised along military lines, able to be mobilised for regional or district rallies. The women's groups were similarly structured for much the same reason. Members had, in many cases, families within the communities, going to school and playing in the streets or fields, going to the shops – these people also were vulnerable.

Visiting Germany, Mosley took Hitler's organising practices as good examples of how he might organise the fascist supporters in Britain. As in Italy, a group of men formed units to act as stewards at fascist meetings to ensure against disruptions. Dressed in brown shirts, they seemed to take delight not only in supporting fascist meetings but also beating up those attending anti-fascist meetings and any socialist or communist meetings they could find. After his visit to Germany, Mosley became increasingly antisemitic, whether because his opinion hardened, or because he thought that the Jews were a popular target, is hard to tell.

In parallel to his political life Mosley also had a personal life, married to Cynthia with three children, Vivian, Nicholas and Michael, and a reputation for being a playboy. During their marriage, she was accustomed to her husband's infidelity, among others having affairs with Cynthia's sister Alexandra, and her father's second wife Grace. Cynthia died in 1933 from peritonitis, leaving her husband to continue in his role as 'man about town', mixing in aristocratic circles and enjoying a bachelor lifestyle. He, somewhat unexpectedly, was much affected by her death, becoming quite subdued for a time despite being in a sexual relationship with Diana Guinness, née Mitford.

Mosley first met Diana Mitford at the birthday party of a mutual friend, although at that time she was married to Bryan Guinness, the heir to the Guinness family business. The affair lasted for a number of years, Diana leaving her husband and renting a house in Eaton Square, close to Mosley's flat. The couple were quite open in their relationship, going for walks and eating out in fashionable restaurants, Diana, it seems, being gradually converted to the theory of fascism and its suitability to the politics of Britain. However, many were of the opinion that Diana had been a committed fascist for some years previously to meeting Mosley.

While Mosley did not insist on secrecy in the relationship, he was concerned that it should not become a newspaper story. Nothing was allowed to disrupt his appeal, his image of the dashing man about town, certainly not his affair with a glamourous, married woman. Certainly his appeal to women members of the BUF was not permitted to be put at risk; whatever the individual wants, divorce and remarriage for Diana was out of the question.

Oswald Mosley saw himself as uniting the different fascist groups and organisations within the country under his umbrella group the BUF and approached them all with a view to their joining him. Many individual members of the BF left that organisation to join him, but Rotha Lintorn-Orman regarded Mosley as too socialist to merge her group with his. However, the BF were near to financial collapse, and she was in poor health, unable to mount an effective defence. Lintorn-Orman was ever the ultra-conservative and saw socialists as her prime enemy. That, and the antisemitic nature of Mosley's rhetoric did not sit easily with her drawing room ultra-conservatism.

The Imperial Fascist League, led by Arnold Leese, was also approached by Mosley about amalgamating with, or joining, the BUF. Leese also declined the offer, perhaps because he felt that Mosley would naturally become the 'charismatic leader' the fascist movement required, rather than he. Leese's brand of antisemitism was the belief that the Jews were an inferior race to that of the Aryans; whereas Mosley's view was that the Jews had exerted undue, and malign, influence on the world's economy.

The entire concept of an Aryan race was, of course, based on an entirely false premise, an invention made to distinguish the white northern European from all other peoples. Although it was an attempt to identify white northern Europeans by virtue of their linguistic origins, it was really invented to prove that other races were in some way inferior. By 1935, it was a concept accepted by Nazi Germany and employed as a term used by white supremacists to justify their claim to be members of the 'master race'.

> Citizenship of the State, and hence participation in the life of the nation, should be denied to all those of alien race, including the large coloured and influential Jewish communities, who should be eventually repatriated to

> their countries of origin or to other countries suitable for settlement by them. Further immigration of such people into Britain should be permanently banned.
>
> With respect to the Jews; our movement, before as well as after such time as it may represent the government of Britain, will be dedicated to the most determined exposure and eradication of their power in our land. We hold it to be the Jewish influence, in politics and commerce, in morals and culture, that is perhaps more than any other single factor responsible for the organised filth and corruption that has infected the body of our society. The removal of the Jews from Britain must be a cardinal aim of the new order, and must be directed not to Palestine – which the Jews have plundered from its rightful Arab inhabitants – but to another of the world's open spaces where Jewish money and Jewish labour will support the building of an entirely new Jewish state.

Very soon after Leese's rejection of Mosley's offer, the BUF decided on positive action to counter the Imperial Fascist League's progress. Making out to be communist sympathisers, they attacked Leese at one of his meetings, and then fabricated evidence to suggest that Leese had plans in place whereby the Imperial Fascist League were intending to attack the headquarters of the BUF. The conflict between Oswald Mosley and Arnold Leese had also become personal, Leese describing Mosley as a 'kosher fascist' and even worse names. Leese was of the opinion that Mussolini had been 'too soft on the Jews' and felt that the BUF was going the same way.

In 1933 Mosley was still following the Italian model of fascism that had been the model for both Rotha Lintorn-Orman and Arnold Leese. With a military structure they were acting as might an army in reserve. Mosley, and a contingent from the BUF, visited Rome to attend a fascist parade as guests of Mussolini.

> Surrounded by British Fascists in black shirts, Sir Oswald Mosley stood in the Imperial Way in Rome for two hours to-day in pouring rain with outstretched right arm, as thousands of Italian Fascists, parading in the Birth of Rome review, marched past. Signor Mussolini himself took the salute from balcony of the Palazza Venezia further on. Next to Sir Oswald stood the standard bearer of the party holding a new banner, presented to the British Fascists by Mussolini. As each section of the Italian Fascists saluted, Sir Oswald returned the salute and the British banner was dipped. German brownshirts watched the parade from the opposite side of the road. After the fascist militia in the parade came the women's organisations and labour corps.

Public meetings in Britain were frequently interrupted by hecklers; one such meeting was held in Bedford addressing farmers. Halfway through the meeting a fight broke out between protesters and black-shirted stewards. In his speech, Mosley refuted the notion that fascism was a foreign concept, insisting that, although it was present in most major countries, the version that he proposed for Britain was in a form that the British would find acceptable. He claimed that the present system restricted agricultural prices, but under British fascism, farmers would receive a fair price for their products. Imports would be restricted, or heavily taxed, and the extra production for the home market would boost the British economy.

The BUF attracted criticism, specifically from one young socialist writing to a newspaper. He writes that Mussolini said that fascism did not believe in the possibility of perpetual peace, and that he believed that war put the stamp of nobility on people who had the courage to meet it, but that Britain had more real freedom than either Italy or Germany in reality. Another correspondent wrote that he detected a growing tendency to edge towards dictatorial powers, while the exact opposite was claimed, and that if a dictatorship ever came to Britain it would be under the mask of the cry for freedom and liberty.

At one of Oswald Mosley's meetings in Manchester where 300 Blackshirts were acting as stewards, a mêlée broke out in the hall, but police were already present, in anticipation of trouble, and cleared the hall of Blackshirts. The fascists still on the platform, including Mosley, were removed, leaving only two men carrying a banner still on view. Eventually calm was restored and these last two were then removed, the entire evacuation being accompanied by booing and anti-fascist slogans. Mosley claimed that his supporters were attacked by a communist mob, the fascists remaining within the law, and that the responsibility now lay with the police, having taken over control.

In a newspaper interview, Oswald Mosley gave his views on a range of issues. Asked about the use of force, he said that although he hoped to attain power though the ballot box, having gained power he would then confer absolute power on that fascist government. If the communists then attempted to overthrow the fascists, they would be confronted with equal force. Parliament would not be abolished but both houses would be transformed so as to support the fascist state and there would be no persecution of Jews – to do so would be alien to the British nature.

One member of the BUF was William Joyce, later to become known as 'Lord Haw-Haw' when he later began broadcasting German propaganda. Born in America (his father was from Ireland and his mother from England), he spent his early years working for the British in Ireland and was suspected of being an informer for the Black-and-Tans, a highly precarious job. He spent some time with Rotha Lintorn-Orman and the British Fascists, and then joined Mosley's BUF at its formation and became one of its major speakers.

Many of Joyce's public meetings involved violence, often finishing with him being charged, along with Oswald Mosley, by the police. He had gained a first-class honours degree from Birbeck College in London and was often billed as Professor William Joyce when speaking at fascist rallies. Without doubt he relished the fighting that accompanied his speaking engagements and, although being described as the director of fascist propaganda, was very much 'hands-on'. Despite his somewhat aggressive nature, he was an effective and impassioned speaker, making endless visits to small town meetings as well as national rallies.

Joyce's fascist rallies always had something of the dramatic about them:

> The meeting, which passed off quite peacefully, was addressed by Mr. William Joyce, the Union's Director of Propaganda. There was no chairman and when Mr. Joyce walked on to the platform, unannounced, a few minutes past 8 o'clock, he was alone. The lights in the hall were lowered and Mr. Joyce, clad entirely in black, with the familiar high necked shirt and a leather belt with shiny buckle, spoke in the glare of the stage footlights, which brought into prominence the two flags standing at the back of the platform against a jazzy curtain—the Union Jack and the fascist standard. Mr. Joyce, speaking slowly and distinctly, but in a ringing tone, commenced his address by describing the fascist creed as patriotic and revolutionary and went on to say that one of the great misfortunes of the age in which they lived was that some of their fellow countrymen were fully persuaded that patriotism was a necessity whilst revolution would be an evil, while another section believed that revolution would be a blessing and that patriotism was an emotion, a sentiment alien to them . . . Mr Joyce described Mr Ramsay MacDonald's views as a hybrid incarnation of Conservative Socialism and went on to indict the government for attempting to hand over India to a small group of Bombay financiers and Hindu agitators.

In rural East Anglia a problem came to light that was not really an issue that ought to have concerned fascism at all, but which given the state of economic unrest in the country gave Mosley an opportunity to spread mischief. Many of the large estates, renting out their farms and farmland to tenant farmers, were faced with death duties to pay. Inheritance tax was 60% in 1934, rising to 70% the following year, significantly higher than the 20% figure only eight years earlier. The only option for some landowners was to sell off parts of the estate to raise cash.

The open market value of agricultural land was relatively low, which meant that individual farms would have to be sold off in their entirety to settle the bill.

Tenant farmers, about to lose their farms, were encouraged to purchase instead. Mortgages were available and the repayments were not too much more than the existing rents. Many tenant farmers took the plunge into ownership. The landowner's debt was satisfied, and the Treasury were in receipt of the taxes. Everyone was happy until the question of tithes was raised, when the new landowning small farmer found that with land came the obligation to pay the owner of the tithe, usually the church, an extra fee. This was not made clear at the time of purchase and was a heavily resented extra expense, for some farmers enough to drive them into bankruptcy.

Tithepayers' associations were formed in Norfolk, Suffolk and Essex to fight the tithe, and some became quite militant, disrupting the bailiffs and the consequential auctions. The BUF, seeing popular unrest grow in the countryside, lent its support to the campaign, claiming that the opposition against tithes was a fundamental principle of fascism. The BUF's main contribution to the struggle was to supply black-shirted stewards to fight with court bailiffs and with the police, stationed to maintain law and order. The show of support from the BUF encouraged recruitment and the 'Blackshirts', shipped from London for the day, were keen to impart their knowledge and experience. While some dispossessed farmers actively sought help from the BUF, others acquired assistance without their consent, even though refusing them permission to camp on their land.

With the BF being disbanded about this time, the remaining members found their new home in the BUF, one of these being Viscountess Dorothy Downe, a landowner with her estate at Hillingdon in Norfolk. Downe took up the anti-tithe campaign with enthusiasm, often sharing a platform with Oswald Mosley and others, eventually becoming the BUF prospective candidate for North Norfolk – never to stand. Downe's social position was a considerable asset to Mosley and the BUF, as she was a close neighbour and friend of the royal family, although the queen did counsel her about standing as a candidate. Unknown to Viscountess Downe, her connections with Oswald Mosley and with Queen Mary brought her to the attention of the security services; her letters were intercepted and her movements logged.

In Spain, the disturbance to the established political routine was also in evidence. The Falange Española had originally been formed in 1933 but had subsequently been amalgamated with another similar group. There were some physical disputes with the socialists and communists, but not on the same scale as in Britain, Italy or Germany, and where the fascists in these countries rallied round one charismatic leader, Spain's fascists were led by a triumvirate, none of whom was to take on the role as leader.

By 1935, Italy was beginning to show its expansionist plans by invading Ethiopia (Abyssinia), and subsequently leaving the League of Nations when it was subjected to economic sanctions. Mussolini's fascists were in control of most aspects of Italian life, both political and social, and the Vatican had regained a little of the status which it had previously lost, but by popular vote re-established the Church's sovereignty over Vatican City. On the matter of antisemitism, Mussolini had always confirmed that his attitude towards Jews, while not entirely ambivalent, was one of toleration and that antisemitic views formed no part of Italian fascism.

In Germany the antisemitic elements of the Nazi regime were hardening and, as Oswald Mosley's BUF moved ever closer to Hitler's version of fascism, so the antisemitic landscape of Britain changed. The Nuremberg Laws in Germany reflected Hitler's views on Jews by withdrawing their German citizenship, instead classing them as state subjects, without the rights of citizenship. At the same time the Nuremberg Laws also placed restrictions on marriage between Jews and non-Jews. These laws were later expanded to include Romani and Blacks, thus declaring them as 'enemies of the state'.

Very few details exist, but it is generally believed that Oswald Mosley and the future Edward VIII met, and had political discussions, courtesy of Lady Maud Cunard, an American who was a good friend of Wallis Simpson. Although Edward did not specifically state his views, it was generally believed that his pro-Hitler views led him to support the BUF and therefore Mosley and his antisemitic views. It has been suggested that Wallis Simpson was sexually involved with the German ambassador Ribbentrop, which would place Mosley much closer to the seats of power and influence than might have been thought.

In considering membership of the BUF there was noticeably a greater percentage of active female members than in either the Italian or German fascist groups. To some extent this can be attributed to the charismatic qualities of Oswald Mosley himself, there being no doubt that many women found him attractive, with his glamourous playboy persona. Fencing was his passion – tall and slim, he excelled at the sport both at school and in the army. He was well travelled and moved in the very best social circles, including royalty, to which he was distantly related.

Although Mosley played no direct part in securing votes for women, it must be remembered that the fascist group founded by Rotha Lintorn-Orman, who had since died, owed a large debt to the suffragettes who had given up their militant activities, at the outbreak of war, to support the war effort. Some had found roles in the armed forces, some in voluntary organisations and some in the

White Feather Brigade. Many had suppressed their militancy for the duration of the war, only to find that their goals were then reached without the need for further direct action on their part. Membership of the BUF offered them a cause to be pursued.

Working class women had also made sacrifices during the war years, not the excitement of militant action, but the security of being the 'little woman', shielded at home while her husband went out to work. Certainly she worked hard within the home, and it was vital she did so in order to support her husband and raise her children. With the coming of war, she was forced not only to run her home, but to earn enough to keep her and her children, and other dependants, from starving. In 1918 this had been snatched away, and she had been left without a place in society, other than as her husband's chattel. If her husband didn't return, she had lost her job and her security. Fascism offered the hope of change and the belief that she could make it happen.

Consequently, the BUF were at pains not to follow the fascist line prevalent in Italy and Germany, namely that of returning women to their traditional roles of domesticity. Instead Mosley offered them the promise of equal pay and greater political participation, terming this as true feminism. While accepting that Britain needed a rising birth rate, to provide a growing workforce, he also realised that women wanted, and deserved, better advice on birth control and many other aspects of good health and well-being.

> In spite of the Fascist and Nazi campaigns to produce families on patriotic grounds, there is a definite and inexorable decline in the birth-rate of the White Races. In Italy, though Mussolini may preach "fertility" till he is blue in the face, the figures are declining . . . In Germany, Hitler has "de-creed" that the birth-rate must be brought up to twenty-one per thousand and maintained at that level . . . Just as Britain "swarmed" in the eighteenth and nineteenth century, so are the races of the East now.

Arnold Leese and the Imperial Fascist League were playing only a minor part in the pro-fascist drama that was playing out in Britain. While the BUF failed to nominate a single candidate for the 1935 General Election, Leese himself campaigned, only to withdraw his name before the election. As well as criticising the notion of democracy, he also claimed that the future of the world lay in the hands of the Aryan race. He claimed that the Jews had used 'finance' as a tool to bring the country to its present state. More chillingly he used the phrase 'lethal chamber door' as a way of ridding Britain of the Jews. He was able to secure a degree of publicity for his views but it was short lived and confined to the provinces.

With Mosley positioning himself and the BUF as the foremost fascist influence in the country, Arnold Leese concentrated his efforts in the provincial, rather than in the national, arena. Leese was happiest away from the London political hothouse, lacking the charm and sophistication of his rival, or the circle of friends that he could call upon for introductions into the highest society. Leese presented himself as a hard faced, hard fisted, fighter – Mosley as a diplomat.

Meanwhile the affair between Oswald Mosley and Diana Guinness continued as an open secret. They were seen together in public and were the cause of much speculation. For Mosley this meant that he was free to pursue other women, which he did with some energy, and maintain his playboy image to the many female, pro-fascist, supporters. He was often involved with the police, being accused of contributing to riotous behaviour, along with William Joyce and others, but received little punishment other than stern admonishments.

Diana, on the other hand, went often to Germany visiting her younger sister, Unity Mitford, who was at a language school in Munich. Diana and Unity both attended the 1933 Nuremberg Rally as delegates of the BUF. Unity in the meantime met and became a friend of Hitler, and introduced him to Diana in 1935, so forming a link back to Mosley and the BUF. Diana, by this time, had become a committed and enthusiastic fascist, and with her connections to Hitler was to prove a valuable political asset to her lover.

CHAPTER 11

RIOT AND ABDICATION

The first major event of 1936, with any direct bearing on the rise of fascism in Britain, began in Spain during the summer of that year. The Spanish General Election of 1933 had returned a right-wing government headed by Alejandro Lerroux. When another General Election was held in 1936, Lerroux kept his seat, but the overall vote returned a left-wing government. Left-wing socialists took to the streets, out of control with the joy of liberation, as they saw it, and the army was called upon to quell the riotous behaviour, resulting in much bloodshed on both sides, in part due to its weak response.

Behind the scenes, army officers began to contemplate a coup d'état under the control of General Emilio Mola. The planned plot became common knowledge but the government ignored the danger, and hesitation allowed the coup to take place. It was partially successful but the prime minister, José Giral, ordered the distribution of guns and ammunition to the population via the trade unions. The government retained, or regained, control of Madrid, Barcelona, and Valencia leaving the right-wing troops to roam free. General Francisco Franco emerged as the leading army figure, and gradually became the de facto fascist leader, being given the title Generalissimo or Supreme Commander.

The country roughly divided itself into two; the socialist government strong in the south, the fascist rebels in the north, with pockets of the two factions in the south and the north. The division between socialists and fascists was reflected in Britain, many young men and women going to Spain in order to join the fighting, while the government kept an entirely impartial stance. Socialists went to Spain in far greater numbers than did fascists, fired by youthful zest and by an intellectually fed camaraderie. Many were university students, others were unemployed and so saw this as an option that would provide a little income and a lot of adventure, albeit at some personal risk.

The civil war had the effect of raising awareness in the British public to the possibility of a coup and subsequent civil war in their own country. They had been aware of the militaristic dress of the BUF for some time, but actual conflict on the ground between socialist and fascist forces brought the possibility home to them. Britain, along with many other European countries, was worried that the conflict could easily spread beyond Spain; many countries signed up to a non-intervention policy to prevent such spread. Britain went so far as to invoke the 1870 Foreign Enlistment Act to make it an offence for the British volunteers to fight in Spain.

In fact about 5,000 men went to Spain to fight for the Republicans against Franco's army. Many were concerned that an all-out fight against the Fascists, if lost, could mean repercussions for Britain. This largely became an intellectual issue, with a large number of university graduates, and undergraduates, forsaking their studies in order to fight – for many a rude awakening. Previously the fight against fascism had been one of protest rather than pro-activity.

Mosley already had an army in waiting, and although there was little sign of dissent at that time, the British Army's loyalty was untested. The government's concern was that Germany's support for Spain, with British civilians involved, could well boil over to a conflict between Britain and Germany. Many British women also answered the call, mainly to act as nurses and ancillaries.

In consequence of the very small numbers of fascists who left Britain to support Franco, little was said by Mosley on the subject, although others were quick to raise the issue of Spain being a fascist state, especially when Franco received military assistance from both Italy and Germany. At this juncture, Mosley was beginning to emphasise the role that antisemitism was to play in his domestic campaign; Franco, although expressing antisemitic policies, was not as well known in that capacity as Hitler, whom Mosley was now attempting to emulate.

> Sir Oswald said that Great Britain was being invited by the Socialists to risk peace on account of the quarrel in Spain. The Labour party had done their utmost to drag Britain into that quarrel. Great Britain was not in a condition to talk of war. "We have laid down the principle that we shall never spend British lives except in defence of the British Empire and not one drop of British blood shall be spent except in that defence." The Fascists would form the closest associations with Germany and Italy if they had government, because that would be a step towards international peace.

Up to this point, Mosley had organised meetings and parades in many towns and suburbs up and down Britain, but he attempted now to organise a London-based rally and parade in the very heart of the Jewish population of the East End. The rally was intended to be confrontational, not only to the Jewish population but also to the communists and socialists that formed a broad swathe of anti-fascist groups. With the anticipated conflict that would be sure to break out, the Metropolitan Police would become involved and, in any attempt to maintain order, would become participants. Mosley would insist that he and the BUF were acting within their lawful rights, while the communists and socialists would insist that their protests were legitimate and lawful.

The rally was well advertised; planned for Sunday, 4 October, it attracted BUF dressed in black uniforms with fascist regalia and banners. They planned to march from Tower Hill en masse and then divide into four separate marches to open-air meeting places where speakers would address the crowd. Although the event was well advertised beforehand, not so precisely the four routes the marchers would take from Tower Hill to Stafford Road, Bow, Bethnal Green and Hoxton.

An organised counter protest was announced, organised by Jewish residents, but gathering protesters from a wide range of ethnic and political groups. Initially the call was to sign a petition, but it was obviously intended to manifest itself on the streets; indeed there were other notices to advise where and when.

> On Sunday, October 4th, the Fascists have announced a four-column march through the streets of East London, presumably in Blackshirt uniform. Mosley intends to speak at four meetings in the heart of East London. The racial propaganda and incitement of the Fascists against a section of the population unless checked, will lead to disturbances and breaches of the peace.
>
> People who have lived amicably together in friendship and harmony with their Jewish neighbours are being incited to hatred, and provoked with disgusting falsehoods calculated to bring strife where friendship previously existed. The fascists are propagating race hatred. They are using the Jewish People as a smoke screen. Behind Jew baiting lies dictatorship and destruction of the liberties and democratic institutions of the British people.

The BUF plan was for Oswald Mosley to address the marchers at Limehouse, Bow, Bethnal Green and Hoxton early that evening. The protesters called on their supporters to assemble in Leman Street, Aldgate, Cable Street and St George's Street in the belief that these locations offered the best chance to disturb the marches.

Police wished the marches to proceed, but with minimum violence; a hopeful stance given that they anticipated a quarter of a million protesters pitted against 5,000 fascist marchers. There were no more than 7,000 policemen.

The fascists began to gather at Tower Hill at about 2:30pm, as instructed, although the first few arrived an hour before that, only to be met with violent opposition from protesters. The police allowed this to continue but, as more fascists arrived, began to separate the two opposing sides, and to clear the streets, so as to allow the march to eventually begin. Crowds began to fill surrounding streets with the aim of supporting one side or the other. Well before midday, a large Jewish contingent of ex-servicemen had added to the confusion by trying to march, and trams had been abandoned in order to make mounted police charges more difficult.

The main confrontation then centred on Cable Street where protesters built two barricades, the first across Cable Street itself, the second at its junction with Christian Street, formed around an overturned lorry. The police had great difficulty in breaching the barricades and were subject to missiles being thrown at them, including rotten vegetables and even the contents of chamber pots. Oswald Mosley arrived at Tower Hill to find the place in uproar, only to be told that his march could not go through the East End, but could still go through the West End of London. This the BUF did, ending the march in Hyde Park.

> The erection of the barricades led to several police charges down the narrow streets. It was half an hour before order was restored. Hours after the march had been abandoned Cable Street resembled a sacked city.... The householders were saying that the Cable Street barricades decided the police to advise Mosley to retire ... Sir Oswald said "If you have decided to ban the procession we accept that ruling. We always bow to civil authority."

There were 150 arrests, nearly all having demonstrated against the march. There were 175 injuries, including policemen and some women and children. As usual, Mosley presented the BUF as exercising their legal right to march, then abandoning the march when so instructed by the police. This was a stance often maintained by Mosley, to push the situation to its limits, to provoke and to be the cause of conflict, but to appear to uphold the law, particularly to follow specific police instructions. It was a very special skill, to be the transgressor, yet be held the innocent party.

A month later the 1936 Public Order Act was passed by Parliament, whereby political uniforms were outlawed in public, and training groups to usurp the powers of the police was made illegal. The Act also made it a requirement to have police permission to organise political marches or rallies. The effect, while frustrating the BUF, effectively made them more acceptable to conservative voters, which in real terms improved their acceptability ratings among the more moderate members of the public.

In the previous month a similar march had also met with large scale opposition when Mosley organised a similar rally in Leeds. The BUF planned to march though a predominately Jewish area of the city, only to be banned and re-routed through another district. The marchers faced 30,000 protesters who, when the speeches began, pelted Mosley and the Fascist marchers with stones. Mosley was injured, and the Blackshirts beat a hasty retreat, vastly outnumbered.

> There were ugly scenes at a Fascist demonstration which was addressed by Sir Oswald Mosley on Holbeck Moor, yesterday afternoon . . . Scores of persons, mainly Fascists, received injuries, chiefly caused by stones, with which the Fascists were freely pelted both during the meeting, and at the beginning of their return march to the city. Sir Oswald Mosley was struck on the body several

> times with stones thrown while he was addressing the meeting from the top of a van. He was also struck by a stone near the right temple as he was marching back with the Fascists from the Moor, receiving a wound which bled freely.

Mosley travelled to Munich on the night of the Cable Street Riot, where Diana was visiting Unity, her younger sister. Mosley was visiting Germany in order to marry Diana in secret, with a special licence arranged by Hitler and guaranteed by him to remain secret. Moseley was concerned about the British newspapers using it against him, to further criticise his record of infidelity, and to comment on Diana's pregnancy. The marriage, now urgent, was to take place in the drawing room of Joseph Goebbels, the Nazi propaganda minister, with Hitler being guest of honour. After the marriage ceremony, Goebbels then gave them, and their ten guests, lunch, which served as their wedding breakfast. It was late in 1938 that rumours were first brought to light concerning Mosley's marriage to Diana, and that Hitler had attended. These rumours were denied by the BUF, which said that Mosley had not visited Germany for more than two years and that any documents must therefore be forgeries – a blatant lie.

Returning to Britain, Mosley and his new wife were then faced with the fallout from the abdication crisis surrounding King Edward VIII and his intended marriage. Mosley had already met Edward before the death of his father, and he was acquainted with Wallis Simpson through Lady Maud Cunard. He was in an excellent position to exploit Edward's sympathy with fascism, and so immediately announced his support for the king and said that he was of the opinion that the proposed marriage should go ahead, a sentiment that chimed very well with his female membership.

The whole matter, although significant in government circles, was not seen as a constitutional one among the general population, instead one of romance and personal freedom. Mosley backed the popular view, to permit them to marry and as a consequence placed himself on the side of the 'common man' against an imperious government. This had been Mosley's technique in the tithe wars of East Anglia, to pander to the popular cause, irrespective of the finer points of law. Again, the general population were not unaware of the law but came down on the side of natural justice.

An unlikely ally in this respect was Winston Churchill, who also came down firmly in favour of allowing the marriage, but in the belief that forcing an abdication would further incite unrest within the country.

> The question is whether the king is to abdicate upon the advice of the Ministry of the day. No such advice has ever before been tendered to a Sovereign in Parliamentary times. No Ministry has the authority to advise the abdication of the Sovereign. Only the most serious Parliamentary process could even raise the issue in a decisive form. For the Sovereign to abdicate incontinently in the present circumstances would inflict an injury upon the Constitutional position of the Monarchy, and cannot fail to be grievous to the institution itself, irrespective of the existing occupant of the Throne.

King Edward VIII did abdicate in December of that year, and his younger brother ascended to the throne as George VI, breaking the well-established tradition of inheritance. The Duke of Windsor, as he was then to be known, and Wallis Simpson were married the following year in France, later to visit Hitler in Germany against government advice. Oswald and Diana Mosley became friends with the duke and duchess, using that friendship as a means of causing further discontent within the country. Strangely, Mosley found himself on the same side as the communists Harry Pollitt and Walton Newbold – all three excluded from mainstream politics.

The effect of the 1936 Public Order Act was that the familiar sight of Blackshirt uniforms was no longer to be seen on the streets of Britain; but not so the fascists. The rallies and marches continued, but in civilian dress, with the familiar faces, speeches and of course the violence from marchers and protesters. Following the Battle of Cable Street, support for the fascists slowly began to decline, but followers remained a powerful civil force, and a constant threat to law and order, not through their own activities so much as because of the emotions they brought out in others. Mosley still organised rallies and marches, but each faced strong opposition and counter demonstrations.

One such rally resulted in Mosley being struck on the head with a brick, rendered unconscious, and being kept in hospital for a few days.

> Sir Oswald Mosley has been removed to hospital with concussion following a skull wound after a Liverpool meeting incident. Sir Oswald was greeted by a shower of bricks when he got up to speak and fell unconscious. A minor operation has been performed successfully.

Then a few days later:

> Sir Oswald Mosley was to-day discharged from Walton Hospital, Liverpool, where he had been detained suffering from the injuries he sustained at his Liverpool meeting on Sunday last. He said he was going into the heart of the country to recuperate. He would not say where. Sir Oswald looked rather pale and drawn, and his head was bandaged. Bloodstains were still on his suit. His mother, Lady Mosley, was awaiting him, and after bidding good-bye to the matron and his nurse and thanking them for their attention Sir Oswald left by car for his unrevealed destination.

Following his marriage in Germany, and his more informal meeting with Hitler, Mosley began to adopt a more antisemitic slant to his fascist message. Mosley began to be referred to as Hitler's puppet, modelling himself on the most dominant fascist in Europe; public admiration for Mussolini was beginning to wane. He was opposed to Churchill's warnings of German rearmament and the war to come, instead supporting Neville Chamberlain's policy of appeasement. His expressed view was that Britain and Germany should never again go to war, one against the other, and that Hitler's expansion plans were to look towards the east, not the west.

Although not actually involved, Oswald Mosley's views were indirectly supported by the visit of the Duke and Duchess of Windsor to Germany as unofficial guests of Adolf Hitler. The couple met many of the Nazi leaders, and had private meetings, not only with Hitler but also with Goebbels, Göring and Ribbentrop, the latter being rumoured to be a past lover of Wallis Simpson. The Windsors were feted by Hitler as though they were royalty, giving rise to speculation that Edward might be in line to become a puppet 'king' should Britain ever be conquered by Germany.

> There was no reason why Great Britain should be involved in war and the blood of the youth of Great Britain poured out in a quarrel which had nothing to do with this country. The Fascist Union had said all along that the Spanish War was not worth a drop of British blood . . . The Labour Party have done their utmost to drag this country into war for the sake of Spain . . . If any nation in the world attacked Great Britain, be it fascist, socialist, or capitalist, then the Fascist Union in this country would fight again for Britain as they had done in the Great War.

With the next General Election due, the BUF began preparing its candidates; among them was Viscountess Lady Downe, now the

Dowager. She had first joined Rotha Lintorn-Orman's BF, staying with it through the General Strike, until its collapse in 1935. She later joined Oswald Mosley's BUF, and then decided to stand for election. Norfolk, where she lived, had witnessed Mosley's attempts to recruit rural support through the Tithe Wars, pitting the farming community against the Church, and it was this issue which was to be the Dowager's main platform in her attempt to be elected, as referred to above.

She had previously been a lady in waiting to Queen Mary and a staunch Conservative. This had caused no problems, but standing for a fascist group had caused the royal family to caution her on the move. Her estate, bordering Sandringham, had created a security issue with the police and she was placed under surveillance, unknown to her, by the security forces. Mosley joined her in meetings aimed at the farming community, promising that with protectionist policies farm gate prices would be improved and would not be vulnerable to world price fluctuations.

In the latter part of 1939 war appeared inevitable, Germany taking more territory by use of military force, finally invading Poland with which Britain had a formal military alliance. The BUF marched through Whitehall protesting over the government's position, claiming that appeasement was still preferable to declaring war, and saying that, should war break out, Germany was better armed and equipped. The Duke of Windsor attempted to intervene by sending a personal letter to the king of Italy urging him to use his influence – but to no avail.

Oswald Mosley urged the British people to realise that going to war for Poland meant the loss of a million British lives on account of people for whom the British cared nothing and that the BUF stood firm against any war except in defence of Britain and the Empire. Should a war be fought, he believed that Europe would then be too exhausted to defend itself from the twin dangers of American financiers and Russian communists. Better that we give Germany a free hand in

Europe, if this will prevent a war, as keeping order in the Balkans is not a task we want. He believed that the British government should immediately say that it was ready to begin negotiations to deal with the injustices of the Versailles Treaty. His policy, as Chamberlain's, was one of appeasement.

The actual declaration of war was made known to the British people on the morning of 3 September 1939 in a radio broadcast by Prime Minister Neville Chamberlain.

> This morning the British Ambassador in Berlin handed the German Government a final Note stating that unless we heard from them by 11 o'clock that they were prepared at once to withdraw their troops from Poland a state of war would exist between us. I have to tell you now that no such undertaking has been received, and that consequently this country is at war with Germany.

Although Britain and Germany were at war, Italy was not immediately involved. There was much speculation, and the fact that Germany and Italy were both under fascist control made its involvement seem a likely possibility. Despite the two fascist countries assisting Franco earlier, there was never any real fear of Spain joining in. Almost immediately after the declaration of war, the Italian authorities declared their neutrality but warned that the matter was under constant review. Fascist Italy, they claimed, had acquired an indisputable title to wisdom and honour, the country had its own problems to solve, but there would come a time when Italy would have its say – an enigmatic comment.

Oswald Mosley, even with war declared, was permitted to continue with his campaign for peace with Germany, calling on the government to arrange a referendum and let the people decide. Immediately following the declaration of war, life in Britain hardly changed, marriages were announced, crimes were committed and trains still ran late. Rumours, however, were rife. Among these was that Chamberlain had resigned in favour of Lloyd George and Oswald Mosley, and that the king had abdicated and been replaced by the Duke of Windsor. It was, of course, not true but was initially believed in Germany where there were celebrations in the streets. Despite official denials, it was some days before the truth sank in and was then replaced by bitter disappointment.

One correspondent posed the question why, when this country is at war with Germany and with the provisions of the Defence of the Realm Act, was the leader of the 'Blackshirts' permitted to demand that negotiations should be opened with Hitler? The answer was not long in coming – he was not to remain free and unimpaired.

> In the last few days we have been shocked to learn that Sir Oswald Mosley gathered an audience in London to address it on the war, and, whether intentionally or not we cannot judge from the brief reports published, aroused a strong anti-Jewish feeling among those whom his clever oratory can always influence. They are not wise people or they would not be ready to believe that 'international financiers' seek profit in wars, which generally spell their ruin, whichever side may win. It is not for us to say whether Sir Oswald overstepped the limits which authority sets to free speech in war-time by condemning our cause and the war.

CHAPTER 12

REGULATION 18B

At the outset of the war, Britain introduced internment for enemy aliens, or those who were thought to be a threat to national security. Initially these were predominantly German or Austrian civilians, living in Britain, and who presented a theoretical security risk. In fact, many of those interned were refugees who had come to Britain in order to escape Nazi oppression, including a significant number of Jews. Each detainee went before a tribunal, to be assessed and then given a rating to indicate their risk level. Category 'A' meant high risk with immediate internment, 'B' meant low risk with some supervision and restrictions on owning a camera or any means of transport, and 'C' meant no risk at all with complete freedom.

Not having been found guilty of a crime, most category 'A' internees were sent to the Isle of Man, where they were held in an internment camp – in reality converted holiday accommodation, of which there was much on the island. Internment began in the spring of 1940 for the members of the BUF and other groups like them. The decision to intern British nationals was not without its critics but public opinion was generally in favour of the government, whose actions were seen as even more positive when Winston Churchill became prime minister later that year.

> No wartime legislation has caused more heartburning and hard feeling than Defence Regulation 18B, whereby a man may be detained and held without trial if he is suspected

> of actions or intentions hostile to the security of the State. Critics have said that 18B – the notorious 18B they call it – has suspended Magna Carta, the Habeas Corpus Act, and every foundation of democratic government . . . It's a question of losing part of your liberty temporarily to preserve liberty as a whole permanently.

Not all category 'A' internees were held in internment camps; many were either sent, or volunteered to be sent, overseas to one of the Dominions who, in return, were preparing to send troops to assist Britain's war effort. Primary destinations were Canada and Australia. This practice was curtailed when the SS *Arandora Star* was torpedoed in the Atlantic while carrying 1,500 German, Austrian and Italian detainees to Canada, together with a crew of 174. Eight hundred men were drowned. The survivors were rescued by Coastal Command and HMCS *St. Laurent* from the Canadian Navy.

> The conduct of many of the Germans brought comments from some of the British troops who were among the survivors. They described some of the Nazis as brutal. They swept aside all opposition in their scramble for a place in the lifeboats. The poor Italians, said one soldier, did not stand a chance against them. When the ship was sinking the Germans made it clear that nobody was going to stand in the way of their being saved. The survivors, mostly poorly clad, are being cared for by the townspeople of a Scottish port, who are providing food and clothing. This food is the first many of the survivors had since the disaster.

Oswald Mosley's position was further complicated by his wife's younger sister, Unity Mitford. Returning to Britain from Germany, she was a committed fascist and a personal friend of Hitler. Her sister

Diana was now married to Oswald Mosley, and the family connection obviously put him under the spotlight. The newspapers reported that, despite her friendship with Hitler, Unity had been denied German citizenship and with the outbreak of war was now returning to her homeland in the face of public anger. Only a year earlier she had appeared at a Labour Party rally in Hyde Park wearing a swastika badge and calling on them to 'save Spain'.

Unity Mitford's return was shrouded in mystery, as at the outbreak of war she was in a Munich hospital, suffering from an unnamed illness. Rumour had it that she and Hitler had a violent argument that either resulted in her being poisoned or suffering a gunshot wound, neither being substantiated in any way. Whatever the truth, her journey home was organised by Hitler himself, first to Switzerland and then by an ambulance train to the coast; at all times she was accompanied by a nurse. She arrived in Folkestone with her mother, who had travelled with her, to be reunited with her father, and then all three of them travelled home together.

After the outbreak of war the BUF was declared illegal and, in May 1940, Oswald Mosley was imprisoned along with eight other senior members. Their offices had been raided under the new Emergency Regulations and he was then taken directly to Brixton Prison. Searches were made of his previous residence in Grosvenor Road and his country retreat of Sanehay Farm in Denham, Buckinghamshire. During that search a quantity of firearms and ammunition was uncovered at the farm. Mosley's wife, Diana, was arrested in June and detained in Holloway Prison, despite her youngest child, Max, being only eleven weeks old.

As they were both detained, he in Brixton, she in Holloway, visits were few and far between. Mosley was permitted the occasional visit to Holloway as a humanitarian gesture. Other than that, spending time together was limited to court or tribunal sessions. Both had lodged appeals against their detention, but both appeals were denied so their separate detentions continued. Mosley and his wife were free to correspond, but their letters were, of course, subject to censorship. Meanwhile, many of Mosley's fascist supporters were released under Regulation 18B as no longer representing a danger.

Viscountess Dorothy Downe, although associated with fascist organisations since 1923, was not detained under Regulation 18B. She was kept under surveillance and her letters intercepted, referred to as being a most fanatical admirer of Hitler, but did not indulge in pro-Nazi propaganda. Being the goddaughter of George V and a one-time lady-in-waiting, there was speculation that her royal connections kept her free. There were rumours that she even attempted to join her friend Diana Mosley in detention, having a letter written on her instructions to the *Times* newspaper drawing attention to the fact that the prospective BUF parliamentary candidate was still free, while others were interned. The gesture was unsuccessful, fuelling yet more speculation.

Arnold Leese of the Imperial Fascist League was a little more difficult to arrest. In June 1940 an internment order was issued, but he was not able to be detained as he had previously set up a series of safe houses from which he was able to publish and circulate fascist propaganda. He was adamant that his loyalties lay with Britain and was angry that he was considered otherwise, regarding it as a slur on his character. He was eventually arrested in November of that year, exhibiting violence in the process and, when finally restrained, caused significant damage to his cell. During his period of detention, Leese went on hunger strike claiming wrongful arrest, and suffered from general ill health; he was finally released before the end of the war on humanitarian grounds.

Although playing a minor role, Unity Mitford was also a candidate for detention under Regulation 18B. Her admiration for Hitler was well known, and when visiting Britain the previous year, she had been forthright in expounding her fascist views. Her mystery illness and return to Britain, with Hitler's assistance, obscured by delay and deception, only added to the mystery. During the period awaiting her arrival in Britain, there was newspaper speculation as to her injuries and these were generally believed to be the result of a gunshot wound. Given reports of a major row between her and Hitler, thoughts turned to the possibility that it might have been by Hitler's hand, or that of his bodyguard.

Later, opinion has been that she shot herself with a pearl-handled revolver given to her by Hitler for her personal protection. She had, only that morning, visited the offices of Gauleiter Adolf Wagner to inquire whether she was to be detained in Germany as an enemy alien. She was told that she was not, and she then walked to the English Garden in Munich, where she immediately drew the gun on herself. Hitler was said to have frequently visited her in hospital and settled all her expenses.

Unity was taken to the Radcliffe Infirmary in Oxford, when she first arrived home, and was discharged from there two weeks later when she applied for permission to live on the Scottish island of Inch Kenneth owned by her father. Permission was refused, despite the authorities allowing other members of her family to visit. There were a number of comments in Parliament as to the desirability of detaining her under Regulation 18B but the answer was always the same.

> Unity Mitford, who attended her sister's wedding in London last week-end, is not to be detained under the Defence Regulations. Announcing this in the House of Commons yesterday, Mr Herbert Morrison said information of her health and the circumstances under which she was living did not give any ground which made detention necessary.

Winston Churchill felt that the Mosleys, being held for so long without charge, constituted a major problem, particularly in the case of Diana Mosley, against whom no specific charges could be laid. Herbert Morrison, Home Secretary, would not order their release, public opinion being against it, beside which the government considered Diana to be the greater threat to national security. Morrison, however, decided on a compromise whereby the Mosleys and some other couples could occupy 'married quarters' in the grounds of Holloway Prison. The pair moved in together just before Christmas 1940, and spent the following two years tending the small vegetable plot they were allocated.

> [When] asked in the House of Commons to-day under what conditions Sir Oswald and Lady Mosley occupied a self-contained flat in Holloway Prison, Mr. Herbert Morrison, Home Secretary, replied that, as detention under 18B was for custodial purposes only and not punitive purposes, he had always had in mind that married couples detained under regulations should be allowed to live together if suitable arrangements could be made. He recalled that it had now become practicable for selected married couples to live together in a mixed camp in the Isle of Man, and said that it had also been arranged for some detainees, including Sir Oswald and Lady Mosley, to be accommodated in a separate block in Holloway Prison, set aside for this purpose. The accommodation consisted of cells, but also a kitchen where detainees could cook rations supplied to them, and two other rooms which could be used as sitting-room and dining-room.

One other consideration was that Diana Mosley, née Mitford, was cousin to Clementine, Churchill's wife, and therefore to Winston Churchill by marriage. Churchill was said to have quizzed Diana over Hitler, trying to understand the man and his idiosyncrasies. Unity Mitford had written to Churchill after the Anschluss with Austria, telling him that the jubilation of the Austrian people was one of the most tremendous the world had ever seen. Churchill replied that he was sure that a fair plebiscite would show that a large majority of the people of Austria loathed the idea of coming under Nazi rule.

Generally conditions in the internment camps were primitive, often cheap hotels or boarding houses, converted to accommodate many more detainees than they had previously accommodated paying guests, surrounded by barbed wire, but otherwise allowing free association. There were problems. Men and women, including married couples, were separated. Jews were housed with fascists, those following strict kosher eating rules sharing the same kitchen space with those who were not. There was only minimal supervision, detainees being left to 'sort themselves out'.

There were riots in the camps; one at Peveril Camp meant bringing in police from London to help put it down. Later detainees dug a tunnel whereby three escaped and stole a boat in which to sail away from the island, but were captured by a naval patrol boat. Other escape attempts were made, all of which resulted in recapture. Generally local residents were unhappy with the presence of detainees on their doorsteps, concerned that they were treated too leniently, given too much freedom and created a danger to the local population.

> Persons detained under Defence Regulation 18B are detained for preventive and not for punitive purposes, and it has been the aim of the administration, in accordance with the wishes expressed from more than one quarter of the House, to make the conditions of detention as little irksome as possible. But it is an essential condition of the greater freedom of movement and association in an internment camp that the persons detained should themselves undertake a large measure of responsibility for the maintenance of good order and discipline. This principle of self-government is that on which the administration of all our internment camps is based.

As the war progressed, and as the danger of invasion began to lessen, so detainees who were less likely to become part of a 'fifth column' were released from internment. Such was the case with Oswald and Diana Mosley, released early on Saturday, 20 November 1943, bound for an unknown destination. There was some speculation in the newspapers that, being unwell, he would enter a nursing home but this was denied; nor would they stay at the home of Diana's father Lord Redesdale.

> The scenes outside Parliament on Tuesday, when Mr. Morrison took the first opportunity to explain his action at length, were in their way reminiscent of the old Suffragette days. The Home Secretary, though taking full responsibility for what he had done, nevertheless claimed to have the Cabinet behind him. He had been guided, he said, by the advice of five doctors of distinction, including Lord Dawson of Penn, and had carefully weighed the medical evidence against considerations of national security. Furthermore he had provided against risk by imposing restrictions which virtually placed Sir Oswald under house arrest. Actually, the ex-Fascist Leader is no freer now than when detained in prison. What then is there to complain about? It is this: That action was taken which not only flouted public opinion and presented Parliament with a *fait accompli*, but must spread bewilderment and dismay among our anti-Fascist Allies everywhere, particularly in Russia. This no doubt was a psychological mistake. But why are so many (organisers of unauthorised strikes, for example), who live in glasshouses so eager to be throwing stones?

Correspondence on the subject was mainly critical of the decision, ranging from those who considered it an insult to serving men and women, to those who felt it would cause offence to working people. Some believed he should remain in detention until the end of the war and then be put on trial along with all the other fascists. One was of the opinion that he should either be released or shot.

When the Mosleys were first released they stayed with Diana's sister Pamela, and then briefly in the Shaven Crown Hotel in Shipton-under-Wychwood. For the remainder of the war they lived, still under house arrest, at the rectory in Crux Easton, near Basingstoke. The seventeenth-century house had eleven bedrooms in eight acres of grounds, plenty of room for the two, plus their sons Alexander and Max, and five servants to look after them all. Their freedom of movement was limited to three miles from the house, with the couple regularly reporting to the local police.

When the war in Europe ended in May 1945, newspaper speculation as to Mosley's future plans was rife, and they had no difficulty in finding those who had been instrumental in the pre-war BUF to provide them with an answer. One former member claimed that the group had held clandestine meetings all through the war years, but was now waiting on instructions from the leader, presumably meaning Oswald Mosley, never referring to him by name. Mosley himself was careful to refute such remarks, insisting that he had no interest in politics and no plans in the forthcoming election, not even to cast his vote.

> Neither I nor any of my friends are taking any part in this election, or have any interest in which party wins. The attempt to introduce my name is an election stunt, which is as silly as it is dishonest. I am at present engaged in farming and writing a book, and have no interest whatever in current politics.

Immediately following this statement, he was embroiled in a prosecution for neglect of his farmstock. It was claimed that he had failed to provide adequate housing and feed for his pigs. The Ministry of Agriculture claimed that Mosley's livestock were emaciated and in a generally poor condition. Mosley undertook his own defence, was cleared of all charges, but received an admonishment from the bench to which he registered his objection, explaining that his pigs could not be better housed as there was a swine fever movement restriction in force. He claimed, with some justification, that prejudice was shown against him because of who he was. Being cleared, he claimed costs, but was denied.

There were warnings in the newspapers that Oswald Mosley was getting too much coverage in the media and there were warnings that extreme right-wing politics, fascist even, were resurfacing now that the war was over. It was pointed out that there was an inconsistency in prohibiting Nazi and fascist organisations on the Continent, yet allowing them to grow within Britain. Legislation was called for but its effectiveness would depend upon the form of words that lawyers could construct to achieve what was wanted, and avoid what was not.

However, by the end of 1945, Mosley was embroiled in fascist politics once again by attending a meeting in London where past members of the BUF were gathered. He was met with cheering and told those who were there that 'the fascists would not forget their suffering and would see to it that their enemies would not forget it.' Many of those attending were in uniform, but this was in private so was not restricted by the 1936 Public Order Act. This was not the first gathering of ex-members; a similar event had taken place a few days earlier and had given rise to questions about restricting such meetings. The response from the government was that although the public felt that there were consequences for those held under Regulation 18B, there were in fact none, and that Oswald Mosley was as free to promote fascist ideology as anyone else.

William Joyce, past friend and colleague of Oswald Mosley, was, at the end of 1945, held in Wandsworth Prison under sentence of death. He had been captured on Germany's border with Denmark, tried in

London, and found guilty. He appealed the verdict on the grounds that he could not have been guilty of high treason against Britain because he was an American citizen, not a British subject. Nevertheless, his appeal was refused and the death sentence confirmed. He was hanged on 3 January 1946.

> Joyce's last visitors were his wife, herself a military prisoner at Holloway, who had seen him almost daily since his appeal was dismissed by the House of Lords; his brother Quentin and his sister. Extra police were on duty outside the prison as a precaution against any last-minute demonstration by sympathisers, but there were no incidents. At 9 a.m., the hour of execution, the spectators numbered about 250. One man removed his hat and stood to attention as the notices announcing the execution were posted.

Arnold Leese, at the end of the war, again took up his ani-Jewish campaign, but extended this obsession by including an anti-black sentiment into his rhetoric. He was charged with others for having helped German soldiers attempt to escape to Argentina, for which he was sent to prison for one year. He again stood trial a year later for committing criminal libel against the commissioner of the Metropolitan Police, but was acquitted. He died in 1956, leaving much of his estate to the newer, right-wing groups, and his house in Holland Park was given over to offices for them.

Diana Mosley's mother and father, Lord and Lady Redesdale, had been pro-Hitler before the war, attending the Nuremberg Rallies and introduced to him by their daughters Diana and Unity. Lord Redesdale, whose name was David Freeman-Mitford, even spoke in the House of Lords in favour of the Anschluss of Austria. Redesdale was in favour of appeasement towards Germany, his wife even publishing pro-Hitler pamphlets. Immediately war was declared,

Redesdale loyally withdrew his support for Hitler; not so his wife, who continued her support but was not detained. By the time their daughter and son-in-law were released from detention, Lord and Lady Redesdale had separated.

Over the next few post-war years, Oswald Mosley was encouraged to involve himself with fascist policies again. His appeal never really reached the ears of his core supporters, the victims of the depression, and those who were living in abject poverty with no sign of escape. In post-war Britain there was full employment, a National Health Service and social security. There was not a common cause to which a fascist dogma might find an answer. The charred remains of fascism had only one policy with which to woo 'the man in the street' and that was an unpalatable one – antisemitism.

In 1948, Mosley formed the Union Movement, a right-wing group which he envisaged embracing the entirety of western Europe, eventually becoming a single state, or nation. He rejected the formation of a federal state, but presented an image of a fully integrated European nation composed, naturally, of Britain, Germany and Italy and other similar countries. In Britain he managed to bring over sixty fascist groups under his Union Movement umbrella, but was less successful in Europe as a whole. Culminating in a London rally of members, and contesting some local elections, success was denied them, and the Union Movement began to wane and ultimately died.

At this time, and with all those who were detained under Regulation 18B now released, many small fascist groups were formed. While many were absorbed in Mosley's Union Movement, most of the others quickly withered in the face of popular resistance. With Germany defeated and Italy being neutralised, they could only offer the negative promise of antisemitism, and the British public, in the full knowledge of the Holocaust, were deaf to that.

Oswald Mosley stood at the 1959 and 1966 elections, but failed to be elected in either, polling less than 10% in 1959 and less than 5% in 1966. This marked the end of Mosley's active participation in the political arena. He and Diana later settled in the French village of Orsay, and he died there in 1980 and Diana in Paris 2003. Comments on Oswald Mosley by writer and broadcaster Malcolm Muggeridge and on his wife Diana Mosley, née Mitford, by Claudia Levy:

> He struck me as being an earnest, rather humourless man; a bit of a bore, but in no way abhorrent; just rather dreary, like a Jehovah's Witness, or one of those figures one meets in out-of-the-way places who produce a cyclostyled plan for world government which they have sent to Adlai Stevenson, Mrs Roosevelt and the late Duchess of Atholl.

> She was the fourth of seven children – six of them girls – of Baron Redesdale, and she and her legendary sisters were high-spirited and individualistic. Their antics made for colourful copy in British gossip columns even when they were youngsters. Schooled at home in a highly insular country life tightly controlled by their unconventional father, they were unleashed on London society when they came of marriageable age and were regularly featured in society pages.

After his death, the family received many messages offering condolences, but none containing harsh words. As for Diana Mosley, who was once described as the most hated woman in England, she also benefitted from time's healing influence and had an equally peaceful end.

CHAPTER 13

END OF THE AFFAIR

In filling the vacuum left by the BF, and Arnold Leese's relegation to the provinces, Oswald Mosley saw his opportunity to come to the fore. This was a natural step for him: his opinions had been rejected by the Conservative Party and by the Labour Party, then by the electorate when he stood for the New Party, a product of his own invention. The Mosley Memorandum, in its various guises, could not find a home in mainstream politics; neither could he. His ego was hurt, his role as saviour rejected, and his God-given right to rule denied him.

It is quite possible that he saw himself as Britain's saviour in the face of division. The country could be said to be indecisive, others might view such inaction as contemplative. To a man who is convinced that he is right, considering a problem from all angles would be a sign of weakness of resolve; a moment's reflection could be a prelude to hesitancy, which in itself would indicate a lack of commitment. Without commitment a movement could not succeed, and without success Mosley would not fulfil his destiny; and his destiny, as he saw it, was to succeed.

His concept for the BUF was that, rather than create a fascist movement by his own energies and powers of persuasion, he should incorporate all the existing groups under his umbrella and inherit an already established membership. With a cohort of dedicated, even blind, followers, he could then take on the role of leader. He certainly had the charisma, the desire to lead, and the ruthlessness to succeed. What he needed was for Rotha Lintorn-Orman and Arnold Leese to hand over the BF and the IFL to him. Both denied him instant satisfaction, she by dying, he by retreating to the provinces.

Mosley's private life was beginning to impinge upon his public life, and when Diana Guinness, née Mitford, became pregnant by him, marriage became a necessity. The connection between the Mitford family and Hitler enabled him to secretly marry in Germany, so preserving his playboy image to his female membership and avoiding becoming embroiled in scandal, as Edward VIII later was – ending in abdication. Mosley's connection with the Mitford family brought with it many complications, not the least being Diana's sister, Unity Mitford.

With Mosley becoming more and more identified with Hitler's version of fascism, he adopted a more antisemitic stance. He adopted the notion of there being a superior Aryan race, to which both Germany and Britain belonged, but he left no recorded comment on the populations of Italy or Spain, the other two fascist countries. The BUF strayed further toward the German model; indeed some members went as far as joining Hitler when war was finally declared, Lord Haw-Haw being one of them.

There was a distinct impression, from his public appearances, that there was a real attempt to ape the image of Mussolini or Hitler in command of his private army. The image of a charismatic leader, with thousands of dedicated followers, many of them women, who looked to him for guidance and political thought. Mosley really did command adoration from his followers, and from his female followers much as a Hollywood star. His very presence could bring a sense of magic to any occasion.

The actual push for power was signalled by an attempt to stage larger rallies with greater shows of force. The Cable Street march, and the consequential riot, marked the start of a serious anti-fascist movement which pre-empted the 1936 Public Order Act and its banning of uniforms. Without their easily identified black shirts, Mosley's supporters still held their rallies, but with less impact than before, and with more voracious opposition. The anti-fascist hordes were more vocal, even putting Mosley in hospital for a short time.

When war eventually came, Oswald and Diana Mosley were detained under Regulation 18B. Instead of being sent off to a detention camp, out of the way of admirers and followers, they were kept in London prisons; not as criminals but under equally strict controls. This was because they were both involved in civil actions progressing slowly through the courts, which sounds plausible, but Mosley had many influential friends in government circles; if not friends – then relations.

Churchill was recorded as being uneasy keeping the two in prison, having been convicted of no crime. So after a while they were given married quarters in Holloway Prison, living much as others who were detained on the Isle of Man. In actual fact most couples detained were never able to live with one another, living instead in near ghetto conditions. Eventually, the Mosleys were released, and allowed to live in rural Hampshire, under supervision. Apart from some restrictions on their movements, the couple were permitted to live quite a normal life.

Oswald Mosley attempted to resurrect his fascist vision after the war, but without much success, finally admitting defeat and moving to France, where he and Diana eventually died and were buried – in a foreign land, not in the British Empire.

Verses by Rudyard Kipling:

God of our fathers, known of old,
Lord of our far-flung battle line,
Beneath whose awful hand we hold
Dominion over palm and pine
Lord God of Hosts, be with us yet,
Lest we forget – lest we forget!

The tumult and the shouting dies;
The Captains and the Kings depart:

Still stands Thine ancient sacrifice,
An humble and a contrite heart.
Lord God of Hosts, be with us yet,
Lest we forget – lest we forget!

Far-called, our navies melt away;
On dune and headland sinks the fire:
Lo, all our pomp of yesterday
Is one with Nineveh and Tyre!
Judge of the Nations, spare us yet,
Lest we forget – lest we forget!

If, drunk with sight of power, we loose
Wild tongues that have not Thee in awe,
Such boastings as the Gentiles use,
Or lesser breeds without the Law
Lord God of Hosts, be with us yet,
Lest we forget – lest we forget!

For heathen heart that puts her trust
In reeking tube and iron shard,
All valiant dust that builds on dust,
And, guarding, calls not Thee to guard;
For frantic boast and foolish word-
Thy Mercy on Thy People, Lord!

There is a final twist in the tale of the rise of fascism between the wars. This revolves around the circumstances of Unity Mitford's return to Britain at the outbreak of war. Unity's fascination with Hitler and the fascist movement is well documented, as is the suggestion that their relationship was of a romantic nature – and by that having an implied sexual dimension. There were also rumours of Unity and Eva Braun being played off, one against the other, by Hitler.

Early reports, as war was declared, were of Unity suffering an unspecified illness while in Munich. These were later confirmed as injuries received from gunshot wounds, following a violent argument with Hitler. This appeared a reasonable explanation considering there was some doubt as to her position in Germany, she being an enemy alien. Admitted to a Munich hospital, her costs were met by Hitler, as were the costs of transporting her and a nurse back to Britain. Her mother and sister met her in Switzerland to travel with her.

The explanation was that she shot herself, i.e. tried to commit suicide, in response to her two countries being at war with one another. The gun was a pearl-handled revolver given to her by Hitler for self-defence. Her arrival in Britain was clouded in confusion and mystery. The party was met at Folkestone by her father, and she was then taken home, or more accurately to a hospital in Oxford. She was handled, as might be expected, as an invalid. Little but her face was ever on view as she was whisked away from prying eyes. A very short time later she was released from hospital, a bullet still lodged in her brain, to complete her recovery.

In 2007 a rumour was voiced as to Unity Mitford's return to Britain. According to one family legend, a small private maternity hospital called Hill View Cottage, on the outskirts of Oxford, had played host to Unity Mitford in 1939. The manager was a Miss Bright, and it was that family legend that had been passed on through her niece. Miss Bright had said that Unity Mitford had actually given birth to a child, before being transferred to the Radcliff Infirmary – the child was given up for adoption.

Further investigation revealed that Miss Bright was indeed the manager of Hill View Cottage at the time, and that Hill View Cottage was a very popular maternity hospital, with many babies being born there.

Is it possible that Unity Mitford shot herself on learning that her child's father had just declared war on Britain?

BIOGRAPHICAL NOTES

ANTHONY JOHN RANDALL

Born and brought up in Bedfordshire, he worked on some of the first computers used in the United Kingdom. Largely self-taught, there being few who knew too much about computers, he worked on mainly technical applications. Living and working in the Geneva area, he and his wife Isabel returned to England in 1978 to set up his own consultancy.

Working on mainly military projects, he was recruited to work on projects that involved high explosives and was asked by the Chinese military to help them with the international distribution of their own commercial explosives. This occupied the remainder of his working life, resulting in Chinese high explosives being accepted all over the world.

He retired to the north Norfolk coast, where he was able to indulge his interest in history and politics by researching both world wars. Prior to this work he has previously published a book on Edith Cavell and her work and execution in WWI.

Anthony is married with two children and two granddaughters.

Tony Randall died on 21st March 2026. His family are all so proud that he kept on working until the end of his life to produce this superb book.

INDEX

Africa 6
Arkell-Smith, Lillias Irma Valerie 56–7
Austria 140–1, 145

Belgium 15, 21, 30
Blackshirts 84, 101, 104, 109, 114, 116, 126, 133
Black and Tans 47, 109
Blakeney, Brigadier R.B.D. 54–5, 64–5, 76
Bolsheviks 53, 59, 67, 72, 82
Boyle, Patrick James 64
British Fascisti 52–4, 103
British Fascists (BF) 55, 60, 62–6, 68, 72–3, 75–6, 78, 82, 84–5, 96, 104–107, 111, 113–14, 117, 131, 149–50
British National Fascisti 55–7, 59, 62–5, 67–8, 72, 75–8
see also National Fascisti
British Union of Fascists (BUF) 100, 109, 111–14, 116–20, 122–7, 130–1, 135, 137, 143–4, 149–50

Cable Street, Battle of 124–5, 127, 129, 150
Chamberlain, Neville 80, 130, 132–3
Childers, Erskine 6, 12
Churchill, Winston 66–7, 69, 128, 130, 135, 139–40, 151
Communist Party 67, 86, 100–101
Conan Doyle, Arthur 4–6, 10–13, 15, 18–19, 33, 39, 43–4
Conservative Party 19, 47, 52, 59–61, 64, 90, 93, 105, 109, 131, 149
Cunard, Lady Maud 118, 127

Downe, Viscountess Dorothy 53, 64, 84, 117, 130, 138

Edward VIII, King 85, 118, 127–8, 130, 150

Fascist League 76, 78
First World War 43–4, 86
Folkestone 19–21, 27, 29, 137, 153
France 16
Franco, General Francisco 86–7, 132

Garvagh, Lord 52, 54
General Strike 58–61, 63, 65–6, 71–3, 82, 86, 104–105
George V, King 26, 30, 70, 138
George VI, King 128, 131
Germany 11, 79
Guinness, Bryan 110
Guinness, Diana, *see* Moseley, Diana (née Mitford)

Hamilton, Lord Ernest William 64–5
Hitler, Adolf 73, 79, 85, 105–106, 110, 120, 123, 127–8, 130, 133, 136–40, 144, 150, 152–3
Holloway Prison 137, 140, 145, 151
Howard, L.A. 55

Imperial Fascist League (IFL) 78–81, 84, 105, 111–12, 120, 138
Importation of Plumage Prohibition Bill 7–8
Independent Labour Party 89
Irish Free State 82–3

Italy 10, 51–3, 55, 57, 71–2, 77–8, 83, 86–7, 90, 95, 97, 103–104, 109–110, 113, 117, 119, 123, 131–2, 146, 150

Joyce, William 56, 114–15, 120, 144

Kipling, Rudyard 6, 19, 44, 151
Kitchener, Lord 19, 22, 31, 38, 40

Labour Party 58, 60, 66, 73, 89–91, 93–5, 123, 130, 137, 149
Leese, Arnold 53, 56, 75–6, 78–81, 84–5, 105, 111–12, 120, 138, 145, 149
Lenin, Vladimir 53, 86
Lintorn-Orman, Blanch 49–52, 57, 104
Lintorn-Orman, Rotha 31, 49–54, 60, 63–5, 68, 73, 78, 81–2, 84–5, 96, 103–106, 111–12, 114, 118, 131, 149
Lloyd George 95, 133
London 1–2, 7, 13, 40, 47, 49–50, 54, 66, 68, 79, 84, 93, 101,103, 107, 114, 116, 120, 123–5, 133, 139, 141, 144–7, 151
Loyalists 64–5

MacDonald, Prime Minister Ramsay 11, 66, 89–90, 93–5
Mitford, Unity 120, 127, 136–40, 145, 150, 152–3
Morrison, Herbert, Home Secretary 139–40, 142
Mosley, Cynthia 60, 89, 91, 110
Mosley, Diana (née Mitford) 110, 120, 127–8, 137–40, 142–4, 147, 150–1
Mosley, Oswald 47, 60, 73, 80–2, 84, 86, 89–92, 94–5, 97–101, 105, 109–120, 122–33, 136–40, 142–4, 146–7, 150–2
Mussolini, Benito 51–3, 55, 71, 73, 77–8, 83, 85–7, 90, 95, 103–104, 112–13, 117, 119, 130, 150

National Fascisti 55
National Service League (NSL) 19–20, 38
Nazism 80, 119, 135, 138, 144
    Nazi Germany 81, 111, 118, 135, 141
    Nazi Party 127, 130
        Goebbels, Joseph 127, 130
        Göring 130
        Ribbentrop 118, 130

New Party 91–5, 149
Nurembery Laws 86, 118
Nuremberg Rallies 120, 145

Orczy, Baroness 24–5
Order of the White Feather, *see* White Feather Brigade
Organisation for the Maintenance of Supply (OMS) 62–9

Pankhurst, Christabel 16–17, 26
Pankhurst, Emmeline 16–17, 26, 44–6
Pankhurst, Sylvia 17
Penrose-Fitzgerald, Admiral Charles 19–20, 27, 29, 44–5
Poland 131–2
Public Order Act 1936 126, 129, 144, 150

Red Cross 18, 23, 32, 46, 54, 85
Redesdale, Lord and Lady 142, 145–7
Rippon-Seymour, Lieutenant Colonel Henry 55–7, 63
Royal Society for the Protection of Birds (RSPB) 11

Scottish Women's Hospitals (SWH) 23–4, 31, 49, 53
Serbia 12, 18, 30–1, 49, 54, 104
Simpson, Harry 75–6
Simpson, Wallis 118, 127–8, 130
Sirius, Captain John 1–5, 43
Spain 86–7, 121–3, 130, 132, 137, 150

Trades Union Council 62, 65, 67–70
Trotsky, Leon 89

Union Movement 146

Volunteer Ambulance Corps 23

White Feather Brigade 21–5, 27, 29–34, 36–40, 44–5, 87, 119
Women of England's Active Service League 24
Women's Reserve Ambulance Corps (WRAC) 49
Women's Social and Political Union (WSPU) 16–19, 45–7